STEPHAN SCHIFFMAN'S TELESALES

Second Edition

America's #1 Corporate Sales Trainer Shows You How to Boost Your Phone Sales

ADAMS MEDIA CORPORATION
Avon, Massachusetts

D.E.I. Management Group * 1-800-224-2140 * *www.dei-sales.com*

Published by
Adams Media Corporation
57 Littlefield Street, Avon, MA 02322 U.S.A.
www.adamsmedia.com

ISBN: 1-58062-813-3

Printed in Canada.

J I H G F E D C B A

Library of Congress Cataloging-in-Publication Data
Schiffman, Stephan.
[Telesales]
Stephan Schiffman's telesales / Stephan Schiffman.
p. cm.
Rev. ed. of: Stephan Schiffman's telemarketing. 1992.
ISBN 1-58062-813-3
1. Telemarketing. 2. Success in business. I. Title: Stephan
Schiffman's telesales. II. Schiffman, Stephan. Telemarketing. III. Title.
HF5415.1265.S35 2002
658.8'4–dc21 2002009993

Ad omnes

Contents

Foreword and Acknowledgments

FIRST, A FEW WORDS ON THIS BOOK'S HISTORY and the purpose of this new edition. Over the decade since this book was first published, it has received positive reviews and has sold quite well. Everything changes, however, including the way that people sell over the telephone. New technologies, improved communication methods, and the Internet have all transformed the way we connect with each other. This book reflects some of the most important of those changes, and I think it will advance your thinking on how to use the telephone more effectively to develop and retain customers. Although the telephone is an everyday part of the business world, it is still seen as an interruption. In fact, the very first stage of growth for a salesperson is that of the "interrupter." That is to say you, the salesperson, are constantly interrupting people with sales calls. The telephone can be the most intrusive medium of all, since a completed call requires an immediate reaction. With the huge number of voicemails and e-mails that we all receive, it is not surprising that many business people feel overwhelmed by the number of messages they must process during a given day. This book shows you how to cut through all the clutter of today's sales world and create a sense of urgency with each and every one of your telephone contacts.

In seminars that I conduct, I often hear salespeople say how well a telephone conversation with a prospect went, or how confident they are that a sale will be forthcoming after a single call. A word of caution on this point: If you have not closed the sale on the initial contact, the real test of how well the call went is not whether or not you got through on the first call, but whether or not you will get through on the second or third call. In a telesales environment, prospecting often does not begin with the first "good" call or initial contact; it begins only when you are able to reach the person on the second call. You'll find that basic principle laid out at various points in this book; it's an extremely important point.

I'd like to take the opportunity here to thank some of the people whose dedication to this project has made it possible. First and foremost, my gratitude goes out to Bob Adams, President of Adams Media Corporation, who has worked with me for the past fifteen years. Without Bob, I probably would not have written my very first book, and I owe him a debt of thanks and gratitude.

Thanks also go out to Walter Gibbs, who has been my editor for a number of years, and who helped me to succeed even with this publication. It goes without saying that my staff at D.E.I. has helped tremendously by putting together various aspects of this book, specifically Brandon Toropov, Martha Rios, and, especially, Lynne Einleger, Steven Bookbinder, and Michele Reisner.

As always, thank you Daniele, Jennifer, and Anne.

Introduction to the New Edition

WHEN I WROTE THE FIRST EDITION of this book, D.E.I. Management Group had shown dozens of sales teams in the metropolitan New York City area how to improve their telesales campaigns. We'd gotten results that made us feel quite proud. The book reflected what we'd trained.

Some years later, when I was asked to prepare a revised second edition, D.E.I. Management Group had shown thousands of sales teams all over the country how to improve their telesales campaigns. We were getting results that even we hadn't expected. (See the case study discussed in Chapter 43.)

Over the years, we learned a great deal first-hand from salespeople who actually made sales over the telephone for a living. We also refined our own training content for salespeople in all business environments (including people who sold for our own company). We did this by:

- Establishing effective benchmarks for tracking personal sales activity,
- Identifying, once and for all, the true definition of selling,
- Determining a strict—but workable—set of criteria for tracking that all-important group of people known as "active prospects,"
- Implementing the Ledge, a powerful new communication strategy designed to turn around initial negative responses, and

- Discovering why someone who uses what we have to offer is far more important than any preconceived notions we may have about "closing the sale."

You will learn about each of these points in the pages that follow. In developing this edition of the book I had two choices. I could:

1. Update and revise specific chapters without changing the original volume's basic structure, or
2. Completely rework the text to reflect the new outline of our telesales program, which I believe to be the very best offered by any sales training company anywhere.

Because so much of our training message now relied on the information I've outlined above, and since none of that information was covered in the first edition of this book, I decided to rewrite the book from scratch.

The result is a considerably longer book, one that draws on a much deeper level of experience than the first edition. This new edition will be of significant practical help to people who make a living by selling over the phone. It features all the key points of the telesales program we've shared with some of the country's biggest and most prestigious companies. To put the matter bluntly: I'm proud that the first book helped so many salespeople—but I'm even prouder of this one.

I'd love to hear your opinion about what follows. Please share your impressions by writing to me at the address below or by visiting our web site, which is *www.dei-sales.com.*

Stephan Schiffman
President
D.E.I. Management Group
888 7th Avenue, 9th Floor
New York, NY 10106
1-800-224-2140

Chapter 1

Getting Started

CONGRATULATIONS! SIMPLY BY PICKING UP THIS BOOK, you've automatically set yourself apart from the vast majority of salespeople.

A few years ago, our company conducted a survey to find out how many salespeople pursue even a minimal professional development strategy. Unbelievably, we found that nine out of every ten salespeople do not even bother to read a sales-related book over the course of a year! What's more, the majority of companies offer little or no formal training whatsoever for their salespeople. For salespeople in general—and for those who must sell over the phone in particular—self-improvement is simply not on the agenda.

So congratulations are in order. You are part of the elite. By opening this book and beginning to read this chapter, you've taken a major step toward assuming control of your own professional destiny. You've demonstrated that you're interested in improving your performance and your career prospects. You've made it clear that you want to learn more about what works, that you want to get rid of what doesn't, and—perhaps most important of all—that you're determined to change familiar (but unproductive) patterns of selling. My hat is off to you.

Let me give you a little background about my company, D.E.I. Management Group, and the ideas contained in this book. D.E.I. Management has trained nearly half a million sales reps since 1979. The program you're about to follow has helped countless telesales professionals to improve their sales approach, take control of their numbers, and increase their incomes. It can do the same for you . . . if you read everything carefully, keep an open mind, execute the to-do items that appear near the end of each chapter, and them *implement* the program for at least twenty-one days after you complete the book.

That last part is important. In selling, or anything else, it takes at least twenty-one days of conscious effort to replace less-than-productive habits with productive ones. If you take the steps I've just laid out, at the end of twenty-one days, you will find that this book has helped you to:

- Develop an effective, personal and professional approach.
- Turn around negative responses.
- Secure more sales.
- Maintain ratios and track your success.

A few more thoughts about this book are in order. We did some research on our audience for this book and found that most salespeople have very little time to spare. We also found that the free time sales professionals *do* have at their disposal typically tends to come in very small chunks. That's why we designed this book to be an extremely easy read . . . something you can look at during your coffee break for, say, ten working days, and complete without having to turn your schedule upside down.

The chapters you'll be encountering are all comparatively short. They're designed to be read in full—and they're also designed to be concise, direct, and to the point. Each incorporates an Action Item near the end of the main text. This is a specific task you need to *do* in order to get the best possible results from this book. Here comes your first Action Item:

Action Item

Set a target date by which you hope to finish this book.

Get out your calendar. Mark this date on the calendar, then highlight the next twenty-one calendar days following. Make a commitment before you proceed with this book to execute the ideas that follow for twenty-one days after you've read the final chapter.

Now that you know what the ground rules are, you're ready to learn what a good sales performance looks like and sounds like, day after day. Guess what? It's not luck, it's not getting the "right breaks," and it's not having a silver-toned Hollywood voice. In fact, one of the most successful telemarketers I ever met was a first-generation immigrant with an *extremely* thick accent. She had to struggle throughout her career to make herself understood by the people who answered her calls, but she posted numbers that made everyone sit up and take notice!

So don't worry about the externals. The key to superior performance over time in telesales is *understanding and managing your own activity*. Let me illustrate what I mean by walking you through . . .

Chapter 2

A Typical Day

EVEN THOUGH I RUN A GOOD-SIZED BUSINESS, I still pick up the phone myself and sell, day in and day out.

I don't generally *close* sales over the phone, but I do initiate most of my new business relationships over the phone. In fact, I make cold calls every day that I'm not training. The telephone is the primary tool I use to generate business. Every single day I'm in the office, I pick up the phone and make fifteen dials; that means I will call fifteen people I have never spoken to before. Now, I realize that's a fairly low number from a telesales standpoint. You may make many more calls over the course of a day, but bear with me. The point is not whether fifteen calls is a lot or a little, but *what role those calls play in my own sales plan.*

Out of those fifteen dials, I'll usually complete the call to about seven of those people. In other words, I get through about half the time. Out of those seven completed calls, I will wind up setting one new appointment. (This appointment might be analogous to a *scheduled* follow-up call in a telesales environment—a call that concludes with both sides agreeing to set aside a specific date and time in order to discuss matters in depth.)

I do this every single day, so by the end of the week, I will have set up five brand-new appointments. In a typical week, I have eight total appointments—the five new appointments that I've set and three follow-through appointments that have carried over from previous weeks. (In telesales these could be people I'm calling for the second or third time to discuss how we may be able to work together.)

Out of these eight appointments that I average every week, I will typically make one sale. Now, if I do that every single week of the year and take two weeks for vacation, I will sell something like fifty new accounts.

It's no coincidence that opening fifty new accounts is my annual sales goal.

Action Item

Identify how many sales you will make over the next nine months if you continue at your current pace and change absolutely nothing.

Get a blank notebook. (You'll be using this notebook a great deal as you move through the chapters of this book.) Use your past three months' activity as a starting point, and *forecast* your sales numbers based on what actually happened in your account base over the past ninety days.

So what does all this mean? It means the *reason* I make the fifteen calls in the first place is not that I have nothing better to do on a Monday morning. I make the calls *in order to generate the fifty sales at the end of the year!*

Now that you have seen an example of the management of daily sales activity and done an initial forecast of your own income, you're ready to . . .

Chapter 3

Understand Your Ratios

DURING MY TELESALES SEMINARS, I usually begin the training session by asking the participants, "Who here has made outbound sales calls over the phone in a previous job?"

Most of the hands in the room will go up. Then I'll call on one of the people who raised a hand and ask, "On average, how many calls did you make in a given day?"

It's amazing how similar the responses are from program to program. First, the person called on will say something like, "Well, it's hard to say. It varied; the total calls really depended on what was on my plate that day." At that point, I remind the person that what I'm looking for is an *average*—so it's perfectly all right that the numbers vary from day to day!

Eventually, someone will come up with a number. It might be twenty calls a day, or forty, or fifty, or some other number. Then I'll ask the most important question of all.

"Okay—now why did you make that number of calls in a day?"

At that point, the participant will stare at me in bewilderment, as though I'd suddenly started speaking Swahili. What on earth do I mean, "why" that number of calls? Is it really that bizarre a question?

Think back on the last telesales job you had. On average, how many calls did you make? How many sales did you close a day? What was the *ratio* of calls to sales on the average day? In other words, how many calls did it *take* you to generate a single sale?

If you didn't know the answer then, wouldn't you like to know the answer now, as it relates to your current job? Think about what happens on the average working day for you. Exactly how many calls will you need to make to close a sale on a given day?

Why should you bother figuring out the answers to such questions? Because your career depends on these answers! Just as my fifty new accounts *depend* on my fifteen calls a day, your income goal *depends* on your own activity and ratios!

Action Item

Make an estimate of your average daily number of dials.

In your notebook, estimate the average number of times you speak to a decision-maker each day and the average number of sales you close each day. Then determine your ratios. Do you make two dials for every decision-maker you speak to? Do you close one out of every sixteen decision-makers?

Once you've developed your best estimate of your current ratios, you're ready to begin . . .

Chapter 4

Tracking Actual Daily Numbers

SOME PEOPLE SAY THAT "SALES IS A NUMBERS GAME." I don't believe that statement tells the whole truth. It encourages too many people to simply "pile up the numbers" without realizing what the various numbers (and corresponding ratios) are telling them. Only by tracking all the relevant numbers and comparing one number to another can we gain any meaningful insights into our own selling process.

Consistency is one of the keys to telesales success. The only way I know of to guarantee consistency is to *know your ratios* and act intelligently on what you see there. Why is it so important to monitor your activity in this way? So you can avoid the classic "ups and downs" of the sales cycle. You know what I mean: Good month, okay month, horrible month, good month, okay month, horrible month, and so on.

Let's look at a typical day in telesales. Consider the case of Bill, one of the managers at my own company. Bill started out in

1983 as a telemarketer. Here's what he had to say about his own early days as a telephone salesperson:

> *When I was in telesales, I'd sit down at 8:30 in the morning, get on the phone, and maybe get a really great call going around 9:00 A.M. Right after the call, I'd tell my friends about how well the call went, pass along all the details to my supervisor, do some paperwork on the sale, and then get back on the phone at, say, 9:30. Then at 10:00 I'd have another great call and go through the same process: tell everyone about it, do a little paperwork, and then get back on the phones until lunch. Then I'd go to lunch. After lunch, it would take a while for me to get going again. Then at maybe 2:00 or 2:30 I'd make another sale. I'd do the paperwork, make sure I'd fax out any rate sheets to other people I'd spoken to, and get back on the phones at about 3:00. I always felt like the people I talked to in the afternoon were not getting my best calls and that I could have been using my time more efficiently throughout the day.*

Have you ever experienced these kinds of cycles in your day? Most of the salespeople we work with have.

Here's another question: Do the best batters in baseball hit a home run every trip to the plate? Of course not—but they do have the same *ritual* for each at-bat. They do all the preliminaries, like adjusting their batting gloves and taking their practice swings, in exactly the same way, time after time. This ritual helps them to execute the same swing—their best swing—time after time. Take a close look at the top hitters during the next major league baseball game you watch, and you'll find that they use the same physical

Action Item

Track your calls hour by hour throughout one day.

List the following columns across the top of a blank page in your notebook: Dials, Discussions, Presentations, and Sales. A "Dial" is what happens when you dial the phone and someone picks up on the other end. (If you sell according to an inbound model, use this column to track "Incoming Calls" instead.) A "Discussion" is what happens when you talk to someone who could actually buy from you. (Monitor these calls, but understand that, in some cases, the first such call to someone won't matter as much as whether or not you're able to have a second call that's just as good.) A "Presentation" is what happens when you make a recommendation to a decision-maker. A "Sale" is an agreement to use what your company offers. Beneath these columns, draw lines for each of the hours of your calling day and use tic marks to track your calls hourly throughout one day. In addition, use a tape recorder to tape your end of the first call you make. Do the same for the first call you make after lunch and for the last call you make before going home. This is an extremely revealing (and important) exercise. Review all your activity; listen closely to all three of your calls. Go over all the materials carefully. Ask yourself when you're most and least effective—and when your "swing" seems to suffer.

approach every single time they step up to the plate. They prepare themselves, over and over again, for the "moment of truth"—that moment when the fastball comes blazing toward them at 90 miles per hour.

People who sell on the phone have to get ready for fastballs, too. And, just like big-league baseball players, they have to achieve consistency. Picture a good hitting coach telling a hot prospect, "You're not swinging consistently. You're not getting the best out of yourself. You're having one great at-bat and then three totally unfocused ones. Take a look at the tapes and you'll see what I mean." What videotapes are to an athlete, tracking sheets and audiotapes are to telephone salespeople.

Please be sure you execute the Action Item completely before proceeding to Chapter 5 of this book.

Once you have completed the Action Item, you will have a better overall sense of what's happening (and when). You will then be ready to learn . . .

Chapter 5

The Five Ways You Can Increase Your Income

By this point you should have actual numbers from at least one day's worth of calls to review. If you're like most of the salespeople we train, you were probably a little bit surprised at the difference between the estimates you developed in Chapter 3 and the actual numbers you tracked in Chapter 4. (And by the way, if you have not completed the monitoring exercises that appeared earlier in the book, please understand that you will not be doing yourself or your career any favors by continuing with this book.)

Let me emphasize again that we must change our activity—what we're actually doing every day—to yield improvements in our actual daily calling ratios. These are improvements that we can track on paper, not abstract initiatives about "doing better" or "being more enthusiastic"! We can't affect our ratios unless we're willing to change what we're doing in at least one of five specific areas.

Suppose the goal you identified in Chapter 4 was to increase your income by 100 percent over the next ninety days. What, specifically, could you change in order to make that goal a reality?

Here's the breakdown:

You could double the number of dials you make in a given day. Theoretically, you could make twice as many calls as you're now making. Granted, it's not a particularly realistic option, but if you were somehow able to make this happen, without changing anything else about the way you sell, your income would in fact go up 100 percent.

- You could double the number of contacts you make with decision-makers. This is not all that farfetched an option. Many of the salespeople we train speak with fewer decision-makers than they could. If these reps focused their callback times intelligently and used voice-mail systems to strategic advantage (topics we'll be covering later on in the book), they could dramatically increase their total number of contacts with decision-makers. Whatever your current dials-to-contacts ratio is, if you were able to improve it by 100 percent and not change any other aspect of your ratios, your income would double.
- You could double the number of presentations you make. In other words, you could develop customized proposals or recommendations for twice as many decision-makers. In theory, if you could improve this part of your selling routine, without altering anything else, you could increase your income by 100 percent.
- You could increase the percentage of sales you close. If your current ratio is one sale for every ten contacts you make with a decision-maker, you could double your income by changing that ratio to two out of ten. Again, I'm

Action Item

Set a target that will help you meet or exceed the income goal you set for yourself in Chapter 4.

Pick at least one ratio from the tracking sheet you compiled. You might, for example, decide to try to increase by 25 percent the percentage of calls you make that result in calls back from qualified decision-makers. (I'll show you exactly how to do this later in the book.) Or you might decide to shoot for increasing the average value of your sale by selling more add-on products or services to the people who buy your primary package. Whatever area you choose to focus on, be sure to set a specific target for improvement in at least one of the following five areas (notice that each can be expressed as a ratio in comparison with something else on the list):

Total calls

Discussions with decision-makers

Presentations (These are formal recommendations based on what we know the other person does.)

Total sales

Value of each sale

not saying it would be easy to do this, only that the ratio affects the outcome in a predictable way.

- And finally, you could double the value of what you sell. If you were able to maintain the same ratios in all the other areas but sell 100 percent more products and services to each person who buys from you, your income would increase twofold.

Now, it may not be realistic to increase any one ratio by 100 percent–but what if you were able to monitor and improve *one or two* of these ratios enough to get you to the goal you identified in Chapter 4?

Here are some even more important questions–questions that should be familiar to you by now: How many calls will you make each day? *Why* will you make that many calls? How, specifically, will the number of calls you make support the income goal you set for yourself in Chapter 4? Answer them before you move on by completing the following Action Item.

Have you completed the Action Item? Please do not read any further until you've identified at least one new target ratio, derived from your own calling pattern, that you want to improve. Once you've done that, you'll be ready to learn why . . .

Chapter 6

Little Things Can Mean a Lot

WE WORK WITH A HUGE COMPANY IN THE MIDWEST that does a great deal of inbound telesales. One of the managers at that company told us that, during the course of an average day, the typical telemarketer in her group would receive eighty calls. Out of those eighty calls, the average representative planned on actually being able to service sixty. (The other twenty were calls that a salesperson couldn't affect one way or the other, such as technical questions that had to be resolved in another department.) So of the eighty people per day that they could sell to, this inbound group was actually selling to about sixty people each day. That was all they had.

As we worked with that company, we found helping the sales force focus on different products and services could help them make a second sales presentation to ten more people a day. Those ten additional presentations resulted in one additional sale per day. This means that when we walked in the door, the daily numbers were eighty inbound calls resulting in sixty sales. When we completed our training and walked out the door, the daily numbers were eighty inbound calls resulting in sixty-one sales.

Now that doesn't seem like a lot, does it? And yet that one extra sale translated into something in the neighborhood of 200-plus additional sales per representative over the course of a year! That translated into a lot of revenue for the company . . . and a whole lot of commission money for the sales reps.

This story demonstrates that even a seemingly tiny change in a telesales salesperson's numbers can be leveraged across all the calls that person makes. In other words, a small shift in the way we do things, carried through consistently, can make a tremendous difference in terms of income.

So we're looking to make any slight change we can—as long as it has a positive effect. We also need to be aware that anything that's not working is dragging our numbers *down* across the board, and therefore we must be willing to eradicate whatever bad selling habits we can find. It's all part of a continuing commitment to self-improvement.

Action Item

Think of the last time you made a recommendation to a prospect or customer that *didn't* result in a sale. Identify at least three things that, in hindsight, you believe you could have done better.

Part of the challenge salespeople face in making positive incremental changes is that positive change *feels awkward* at first. Read on to learn why incorporating good selling habits is like perfecting . . .

Chapter 7

Your "Golf Grip"

THERE'S AN INHERENT PARADOX at work whenever we attempt to improve sales performance.

Our ultimate goal is to be consistent, to straighten out the line, to approach each call with our very best "home run swing." But, in order to be consistent, we have to change. We have to try different things, identify what works, and build it into our routine so we don't fall back into old, unproductive habits.

Successful salespeople don't sit down at a desk from nine to five just to follow instructions and do paperwork. They take conscious control of their day. They take personal responsibility for both their actions *and the outcomes of those actions*. They think about what they are doing *and what they must do differently* in order to be more successful.

Successful salespeople consistently do those things that elevate themselves above the norm . . . even if that means updating and improving a familiar routine.

The key to making positive change in your phone sales routine is to find something you want to change and then practice it over and over and over again until you're consistent in the new habit. Yet the very first time you *start* doing things in a different and more efficient way, you're likely to feel awkward and uncomfortable.

I once took golf lessons from a pro. The pro handed me a golf club and showed me all the elements of the proper grip. It felt quite strange. Then he showed me how to stand, how to swing, how to follow through. Everything he asked me to do felt awkward. I swung, just as he'd instructed me, and it felt totally uncomfortable. The pro left and told me to continue practicing. I practiced for a few hours, but I found that when I moved my grip to a more comfortable position, I could still hit the ball. I also found that when I moved my feet so that they didn't feel as awkward, I could still hit the ball. So I forgot about the lessons and started playing golf "my way," which translated to an average score of 150 in nine holes. I wasted a whole year feeling "comfortable." Eventually I had to track down the pro and take the lessons all over again.

The ideas you encounter in this book may feel awkward at first, but if you stick with them and *implement them* for the twenty-one days you've committed to, you will improve your performance. I don't want you to waste a year, the way I did, with a "comfortable grip." I want you to master the *right* grip. As you close out this chapter, be sure you're making every possible incentive work for you. So please execute the Action Item at the end of this chapter—which will help you define and commit to a motivating goal—before you move forward to Chapter 8.

Action Item

Set a new income goal for yourself.

Write your new goal down in your notebook. It should take the form of this sentence: "By [date], I will earn a total of [amount] in salary and commissions by increasing my telephone sales effectiveness and developing more satisfied customers." Be sure the date you choose is no more than ninety days away. Be sure the amount you choose is no less than 15 percent higher than the amount you earned over the most recent equivalent period. Post this sheet of paper in a spot where you will see it at least three times a day without meaning to. On a separate sheet, write down at least ten ways your life will improve by attaining this goal. Be as specific as you possibly can. By identifying a clear goal, specifying the date of its attainment, and visualizing the benefits clearly, you will give yourself an incentive to "stick with the program" even though doing so may feel awkward or unusual at first.

Now that you know why consistency requires change and you're equipped to handle the awkwardness you may feel when you try to alter your existing routine, let's move on to the most misunderstood concept in all of sales. I'm speaking, of course, about . . .

Chapter 8

"Closing" (And Its Hazards)

PLEASE NOTICE THE QUOTATION MARKS in the title of this chapter.

Those of us who sell for a living are accustomed to talking about "closing" deals. We're so accustomed to this, in fact, that I employ the term, in a general descriptive sense, in all our training programs. And yet I'm not sure that "closing" is really the best idea for us to focus on as we think about the selling process.

If you think about it, our real objective in the sale is not to "close" anything, but to get people to *use* our service and to continue to do so forever. That sounds more like an opening than like a closing, doesn't it?

So let's dig a little deeper. What we really want to do is come up with a *plan that will make sense* to the prospect—so he or she will actually *decide* to use our services. That makes a lot more sense than focusing on what we imagine the person "needs." Instead of getting distracted by what we assume (usually incorrectly) the person needs, we're better off building our plan around what the person *does*. And here we come to the key idea behind this program.

The key to getting results from this book lies in engaging prospects and customers in conversations that illuminate what they actually do. This is the only way to develop a presentation that will help the other person do what he or she does better. The focus really isn't on "closing" people, but on finding out . . .

- What they do,
- How they do it,
- Why they do it,
- When they do it,
- Where they do it,
- Who they do it with, and
- How we can help them do it better.

In fact, that's our *definition* of selling. Focusing on the "do" in this way is the activity most likely to result in a plan that will cause the other person to decide to *use* what we have to offer. That's why the "do" is so important. It makes your presentation—your plan—*relevant* to the prospect. Your recommendation is customized, not something that is targeted to the general population. We estimate that 90 percent of all sales that are lost are lost because salespeople fail to understand the "do."

In reality, people don't buy because of what we think they "need"—they buy because it *makes sense* to them to do so, based on what they're trying to accomplish at any given point in time.

So here's a quick recap: Trying to "close" the sale based on what we think the person "needs" is a waste of time and effort. We are developing a plan meant to get people to *use* our service (forever, we hope) because it MAKES SENSE to them to do so. And the only way to build a plan that MAKES SENSE for these people is for you to find out exactly what they're trying to do! To do that, you have to get information about the prospect.

Action Item

On a blank page in your notebook, write the following phrase in huge letters: "THE 'CLOSE' IS REALLY THE 'USE.'"

We've seen how important it is to get information about *what your prospect is doing now*. Continue on to the next chapter to find out how that essential task is one of . . .

Chapter 9

The Four Steps of the Telephone Sales Process

YOU JUST LEARNED THAT FINDING out what the person does is essential to putting together your plan for that person. But at what point in the phone call do you find that out?

Let's look at how the four steps of the telephone sales process actually work. Here's an illustration to consider.

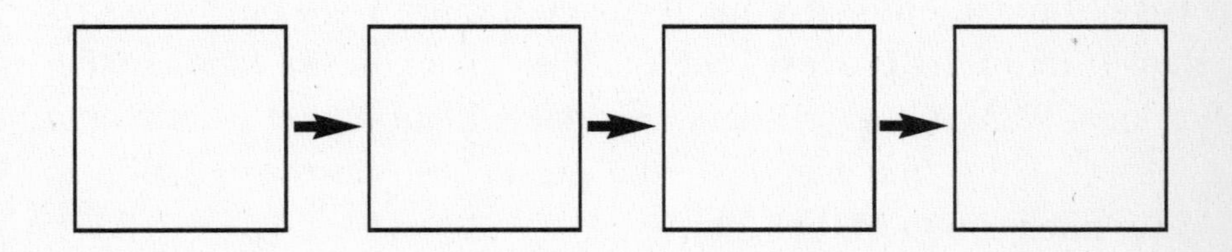

What would you say is the objective of the first step?

When I ask this question during training seminars, here are the answers I get: "To open the relationship." "To generate rapport." "To develop good personal chemistry."

All these answers miss the point. The correct response is much more straightforward. The goal of the first step is simply *to get to the Next Step!*

Look at the diagram once again, this time with a little more information about what occurs within each of the steps.

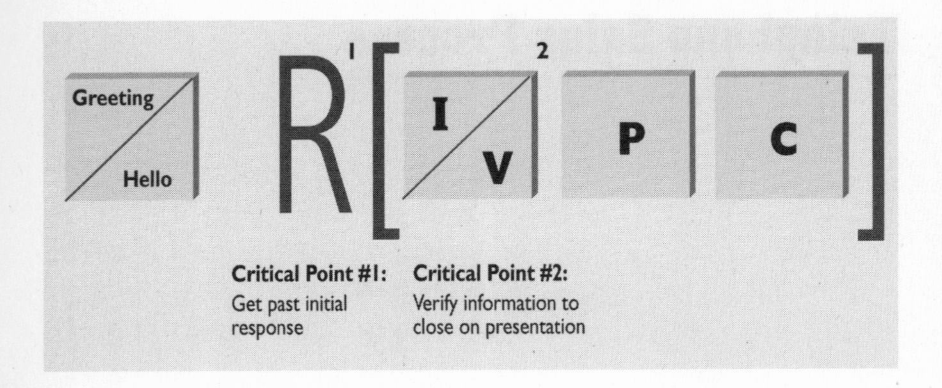

The steps, in order, are opening (also known as qualifying), information-gathering, presentation, and closing. We greet the prospect and we get a response—typically a negative response such as "I'm not interested." We can *only* move on in the sales process if we get *past* that first response, or Critical Point—otherwise, the call ends. It would be nice if there were only one Critical Point in the process, but it is likely that you will face another Critical Point in the presentation phase. Right now, I want you to focus on the *first* response, the person's instinctive reaction to your interruption of their day.

It's a fact of life: When we make a telesales call, we must expect the other person to try to cut the call off with an initial negative response. That first response is going to come at us so fast that we're going to have to be prepared for it, and we're going to have to develop a strategy for turning it around so we can move forward in the process. A little later in the book, you'll get the ammunition you need to turn around the responses you receive at Critical Point #1 *and* Critical Point #2.

If we can turn around that first response, then we can move into the rest of the call—information-gathering (where we interview the prospect in order to put together the right plan), the presentation (where we make our recommendation and offer a *reason* to work with us), and the close (where the person decides to *use* what we have to offer). The second step of the sales cycle—the information-gathering step—is the make-or-break part of the relationship. Now, at D.E.I. we look at the information step a little differently than other training companies do. Other sales training firms look at this step as a chance to find out what the prospect's "needs" are. It should be clear to you by now that we take a very different approach. We feel the truth is that not enough people actually need our product or service *at the time we need to make a sale.* So the key word, for us, is not "need" but "do."

Let's assume it's your job to place outbound sales calls. If the prospect really "needed" your product or service, wouldn't he or she be calling you up trying to buy it?

Suppose you're taking *inbound* calls. If you're doing more than simply taking orders—that is, if you're functioning as a salesperson rather than a customer service professional—how can you increase the value of the account? Can you really do that by focusing on your own preconceptions about what the person "needs"? What if that doesn't match up with what the customer or prospect thinks he or she needs? When does the event that inspired the person to *call you in the first place* come into the equation?

Action Item

Complete the following mini-quiz.

What is the first obstacle you are likely to face in progressing to the second stage of the sales process—the information-gathering part of the conversation where you find out what the other person does? Please write your answer in your notebook.

You'll find the answer printed upside down at the bottom of this page. Once you've checked yourself, move on to the next chapter and understand the importance of refining your selling approach. You'll do this by taking a trip to . . .

The initial negative response, also known as Critical Point #1

Chapter 10

Understand the Numbers—and Improve Your Approach

DO YOU KNOW YOUR NUMBERS?

Imagine you're in Times Square in New York City—one of the busiest city centers in the world. Suppose you were to stand there on the corner and simply hold out your hand. Do you think anybody would put money in your hand? Sure. Eventually, someone would give you some money, just because you held your hand out.

Now suppose that, instead of just standing there with your hand out, you held out a big, brightly colored cup. Do you think you would make more money with that approach? Sure you would.

Suppose that, instead of just holding your hand out and holding a cup, you used a bell to attract attention. You'd make more money still, wouldn't you? Then suppose you added a sign that said "Please help me." Do you think you would make more money? Yes, you would.

What if you had a cup, a bell, and a sign, and you started walking up to people and saying, "Can you help me?" Do you think you'd make more money? *Of course* the answer is yes—but the real question is why? Why, in each of these scenarios, did you make more money? The answer is that each time you changed your approach and enhanced what you were doing.

I know of a man who sells business card cases in New York City by simply standing at the subway entrance and saying, "Want to buy, want to buy, want to buy?" That's all he does. Just stands there and repeats that phrase: "Want to buy?" At the end of the day his chauffeured Rolls Royce drives by and picks him up! What has he learned?

This man has come to the realization that 42 million people are going to walk past him every year, and if he stands there long enough, EVENTUALLY someone is going to buy from him. *He understands his numbers.*

You could sell that way too, by simply putting your hand out and waiting . . . but unfortunately you don't have an audience of 42 million people! You can, however, make a conscious choice to enhance what you're doing. You can improve your ratios by improving your approach on the phone, by spending less time with people who *aren't* willing to move through the sales process with you, and by making a conscious choice to manage your ratios effectively over time. The end result will be that more people will actually decide to *use* what you have to offer.

Action Item

How many total dials will you make over twelve months, based on the numbers you developed in Chapter 5? Write the answer in your notebook.

Keep reading to find out how to . . .

Chapter 11

Move Forward in the Sales Process

ONCE UPON A TIME, a salesperson called a decision-maker. The two of them had a "great conversation" that lasted over twenty minutes. As this call unfolded, the salesperson felt the conversation was great. The prospect said the conversation was great. The sales manager listened in for a while to the representative's side of the call; even he agreed it was a great conversation.

In short, *everyone* thought this was a great call. After twenty minutes, the prospect said, "This was great; now I know everything about you and your company that I could possibly want. We don't need to speak anymore. Please don't ever call me again." And with that, the person hung up.

Was that really a great call? Of course not. But *why* wasn't it a great call?

Because the sales rep was not able to move to the Next Step with the prospect! A Next Step is an unmistakable commitment of time and attention, in the short term, that both sides agree to.

It involves specific date and time.

Actually, if you leave out the part about the twenty minutes she could have spent doing something else, this salesperson was actually quite lucky. At least she knew exactly where she stood at the end of the call!

Many of the people we call on the phone won't come out and tell us "Please don't ever call me again." Instead, they'll say things like this: "I'll think about it," or "I don't have time," or "I'll have to check with somebody else." But if what they say doesn't translate to a Next Step, we really have nothing. We aren't moving forward in the sales process—even if we think the other person "needs" what we have to offer.

At the risk of repeating myself, let me remind you again that what really matters is *not* what we think the prospect "needs" but what the person actually *does*. In fact, the number one competitor any salesperson faces is not any particular company, but the *status quo*—what the prospect or customer is already doing. People don't "need" to change what they are currently doing because what they're doing already makes sense to them. How do we *know* it makes sense to them? They're still doing it!

If you walked into someone's office and saw a huge brown cow sitting in the corner, munching away at the carpet, your first question would probably be the obvious one: "Gee, why do you have a brown cow in the office?" Yet most telemarketers are perfectly happy to talk for half an hour with a prospect without asking an equally obvious question: "Gee, I'm just curious, why are you with XYZ Company?" It's questions like these that help us identify opportunities to find out what the person is doing (and why) and move forward in the sales process.

But most salespeople don't bother asking questions like this. Let's look at how the typical salesperson sells. There is usually a big opening/presentation. (At my company, we call this "throwing up" all over the person we're talking to.) Then the salesperson asks a few listed questions and then makes a big presentation with three options and tries to utilize one of the 187 prescribed closes. The presentation is about 90 percent of the sale—but it takes into account very little information about the prospect. And it's usually a struggle, because the other person is busy firing off reasons why the call should actually be over.

What most salespeople call "objections" at the outset of the call are really instinctive, "knee-jerk" responses by the prospect. As we've seen, this initial negative response is Critical Point #1 in the outbound call. We can't move on until we get past that first response. You'll get specific strategies on how to turn around negative responses in Chapters 24 through 29. For now, understand that you *will* have to find ways to turn these responses around. There's no reason to be surprised when you run into this resistance.

It's important not to mistake these instantaneous responses (such as "I have no interest" or "We're all set") as rationally structured, reasoned arguments against our product or service. Actually, they're simply a predictable part of a larger process in which a certain percentage of prospects will eventually *agree to move forward with us through the steps of the sale.*

Selling over the telephone is really a series of steps, each of which leads to the next. If you don't get your prospect to the steps with you, you can't make a sale; if we do not find a way to turn around the initial response and move through the process, we are not yet talking to an actual prospect.

Look again at the four steps of the ideal selling cycle.

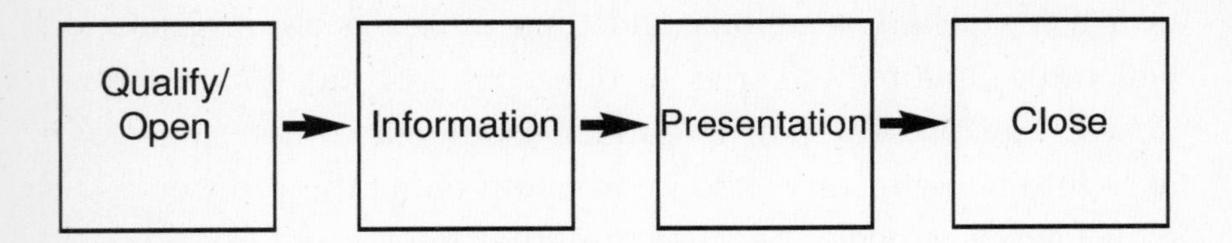

Q stands for Qualifying/Opening the relationship. I stands for Information-gathering or Interviewing, getting information. P stands for Presenting, or the Plan that we use to identify the REASON that it makes sense for the person to use what we have to offer. C stands for Closing the sale. (We use the term "Closing" because it's familiar to salespeople, but in fact what we're doing is developing a plan that makes sense to the other person and inspires him or her to *use* what we have to offer.)

This time, you'll notice, our boxes are different sizes because in our sales model 75 percent of the sale is completed prior to the presentation. This is because if the interview is thorough, the proper presentation will "make sense" and will be more likely to close. In fact, the way you will close the sale over the phone is simply by asking the customer, "Makes sense to me, what do you think?"

There are really only two ways a prospect can react to this question. The person will either say, "Yes, it does make sense," in which case the sale closes, or the person will say, "No, it really doesn't make sense to me." Then there's a great opportunity to find out exactly what's going on. All you have to do is ask, "Really? Why not?" The most amazing thing happens when you ask this kind of question. You get an answer!

When the other person tells you why what you've proposed doesn't make sense, what he or she will actually be telling you is what is wrong with your proposal. In telling you what's wrong with the proposal, the person is actually showing you how to make it right. You don't have to be right all the time; you simply have to be willing to be righted . . . and keep the relationship alive.

Action Item

Identify the two most common knee-jerk responses you can turn around.

In your notebook, make a list of the most common initial "knee-jerk" responses you hear from the people you call. Place a check mark by the *two* responses you would most like to be able to turn around easily . . . two responses that are now preventing you from learning about the other person and moving forward in the sales process.

Once you've identified at least two of these "automatic" responses, turn to Chapter 12 to find out why you must . . .

Chapter 12

Define Prospects Accurately

MOST SALESPEOPLE ARE UNDER THE IMPRESSION that they have far more prospects than they actually do. This is because they use an open-ended, essentially meaningless definition of the word "prospect." For most people, a prospect is simply "someone who will pick up the phone when I call" or even "someone with whom I hope to do business eventually."

In order to develop a more pragmatic definition of a prospect, we must quickly review a few key points.

What's the objective of the first step of the sales process? You know the answer: It's to get to the second step. And the goal of the second step? To get to the third. And the objective of the third step? You guessed it. It's to get to the fourth and final step, the "close" (to use the most popular terminology), where the person decides to *use* what we have to offer. Essentially, selling in a telesales environment is simply a series of steps. And this series of steps takes place over a certain period of time–whether that's one call or a number of calls–with each step bringing you closer to a commitment.

All of this brings us to our *definition* of a prospect. A prospect is someone who has shown a willingness to advance through each step of the sales cycle with you *and* to do so within your "normal" time frame. If there's no commitment to work through the process within that time frame, then there's no prospect. In many instances, I've found that salespeople in an outbound telesales environment are well advised to consider no one a prospect unless that person has taken part in *two* good conversations. That's evidence that the person is truly "playing ball" with you.

You'll notice that, in defining the prospect, I've touched on the concept of time. Let's look at that idea in a little more depth. As I go through each step in the sale, I know that time is passing. I know that my sale, on average, takes about eight weeks to move all the way from the first step to the fourth step. (If your sale happens in a telesales environment, odds are it will move more quickly than that.) But what happens to my chances of closing the sale if the time factor is *longer* than normal–if it goes beyond that average amount of time?

The answer is simple: My chances of completing the sale decrease. The longer I go past my average, the lower my chance of closing the sale.

Suppose someone you're talking to tells you, "Call me back in six months and we'll look at this again." Have you really gone to the Next Step with that person? What do you think will actually happen in six months? Do you imagine that, that morning, your contact is going to spring out of bed, run to the calendar, and say, "Yes! Today's the day! I can expect a call!" I hope you'll agree with me that the chances for that are slim.

It may take you an average of one call or an average of four calls or an average of six calls or an average of twenty calls to close a sale. My point is that you must *know what that number is and know when your contacts have exceeded it.*

Let's say that your norm is three phone calls, placed over a period of two weeks, before you reach the fourth ("closing") step. And let's say you're talking to someone for the twentieth time. You should know this contact is well beyond your norm and is highly unlikely to turn into revenue for you. The sad truth is that this person is probably not moving through the sales process with you at all. You have, in all probability, simply hooked up with someone who enjoys having someone to talk to on the telephone. (It happens.) In such a case, you do not have a prospect; what you have is an *opportunity* for future business.

So what have we learned? When someone is *actively* moving through the sales process with you *in a time frame that matches your average selling cycle,* that person is a prospect. When someone is *not* actively moving through that cycle within that familiar time frame, it makes more sense to classify that person as an opportunity, not a prospect.

This definition means that we classify people who schedule Next Steps with us *differently* than people who don't. We make a conscious choice to treat someone who says "Yes, I'll talk to you next Monday at 1:00" as a higher priority than someone who says "Look, it sounds interesting—call me sometime next week." The first person is "playing ball" with us. The second person isn't!

Perhaps you're asking yourself: Why is that kind of specific commitment such an important thing? Well, think about your own priorities. I'm willing to bet that you have a Day Timer or a kitchen calendar at home. Whatever you call it and wherever you keep it, the odds are that you have a "house calendar." Now, think for a moment about what actually gets onto that personal calendar. Is it always your *favorite* activities? Occasionally, but if you actually look at the entries, you'll find that this calendar typically tracks things like dental appointments, getting the car fixed, taking the dog to the vet, and so on. These are important events—events that you might not necessarily rank as your favorite things to do but that have to get done nonetheless. And if something's on that calendar, it's more than likely that it's going to happen. In other words, if there is a conflict between wanting to take a nap and going to a dental appointment you scheduled two weeks ago, the dental appointment is more likely to happen, even though the nap might seem more preferable at any given moment.

Action Item

Review your "top prospects" and their movements through the sales process.

Review your calling records and make an estimate of the average number of calls it takes you to close a sale. Record this number in your notebook. Then review those contacts you now consider "top prospects" and ask yourself: How long have I been talking to each of these people? How many of these relationships now *exceed* my average sales cycle length? How many of these people have scheduled a clear Next Step with me?

That's the way it works in our life, and that's way it works in our customer's life, too. Just like us, our customers have a long list of things they'd *like* to do. But there's a shorter list of important things that they will actually *schedule and commit to doing.* So if Mr. Jones will schedule a time to speak to me again, that's very significant. That means that this person has actually made a commitment to move through the sales process with me. I want to identify *everyone* who falls into that category!

The point I'm making in this chapter is vitally important, even though it may seem at first to represent a mere quibble over words. *Identifying those people who are moving through the process with you* is anything but a semantic game. This will become clearer to you as you come to understand the remarkable power you possess *right now* to use questions to focus the conversation and summon your power to move the right relationships forward. In order to put that power to work over time, you must learn to . . .

Chapter 13

Count the "No" Answers

AT D.E.I. WE HAVE TRAINED OVER 9,000 SALES ORGANIZATIONS around the world in virtually every industry you can name. That kind of experience has given us the opportunity to put together some real-world averages that can be quite helpful in evaluating selling ratios.

What we've found is that, as a general but fairly reliable rule, twenty calls will typically yield five prospects within an effective sales organization. (If you are at all uncertain about what constitutes a prospect, please reread Chapter 12!) Those five prospects will typically yield a single sale.

These numbers have been proven out in a variety of industries and selling environments. Look at them once again:

20:5:1

We will step in front of a group of sales representatives in a sales training program and say, "Look at these ratios: Twenty calls give you five prospects, and five prospects give you one sale. How many 'no' answers do you see in this equation?"

Some reps only see four "no" answers; some see fifteen. In fact, there are *nineteen* "no" answers along the road to a typical sale. What's interesting about this is that most salespeople never count the number of "no" answers they receive and thus have no idea how their own performance stacks up next to the averages we've identified!

Pretty amazing, isn't it? The average salesperson can tell you how many sales he or she made last week, last month, or last quarter; what all the relevant figures were on the W2 last year; what his or her base salary and pay grade is; what the commission percentage is; and so on. Most salespeople can even tell you how many miles they have to drive to the office every day! But if you ask those same people how many companies they had to call to generate a single sale, all that comes back is a blank stare. That's what I call the curse of the average salesperson.

Don't be the average salesperson. Count the number of "no" answers you receive. Identify the exact number of "no" answers it takes you to get a sale. Know whether you're getting enough "no" answers any given day, week, or quarter. Figure out the numbers, if only for the sake of your own career! If you don't understand "no" answers for what they are, your performance—and your outlook on your job—will suffer.

The key here is to *count the "no" answers.* Don't just count the "yes" answers. It's easy to forget that each "no" answer is part of the process by which you receive income. Actually, each time someone tells you "No, thanks," you've earned a portion of your annual income. The question is, how much? If you count the "no" answers, you'll know.

Many, many sales reps fall into the "time and money" trap. Take a look at the following graph.

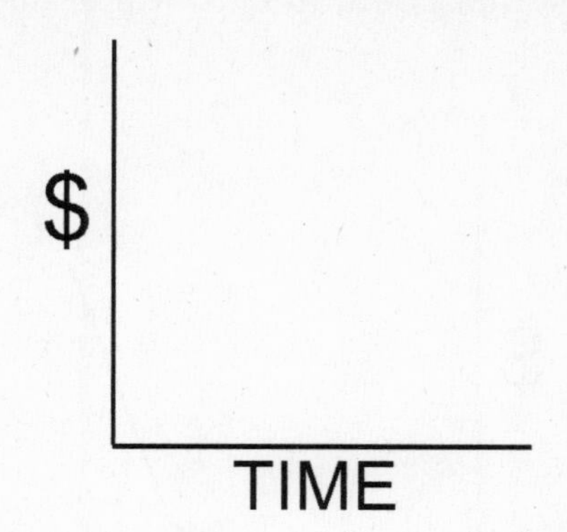

One line represents time; the other represents money. Often, salespeople will go through an initial period in their positions when they *seem* to be getting an awful lot of "no" answers without enjoying any significant return for their effort. They hear "no" after "no" after "no"—and they quit right before the point where they've started to amass enough "no" answers to yield some real income.

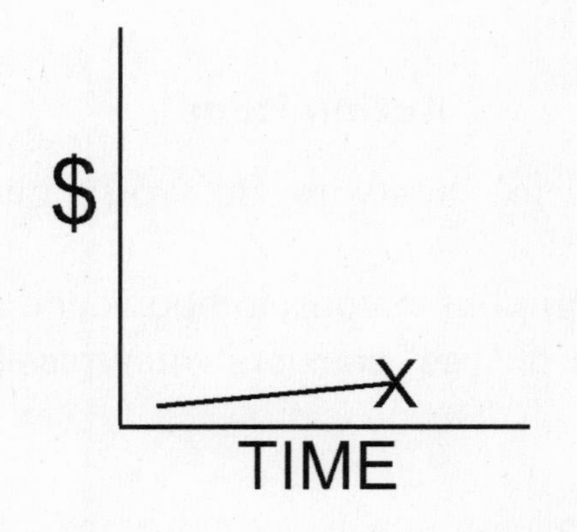

They quit right where the X is in the above graph. That's the point where all the "yes" answers were about to start coming in.

If they could get past that point, here's what their income picture would look like:

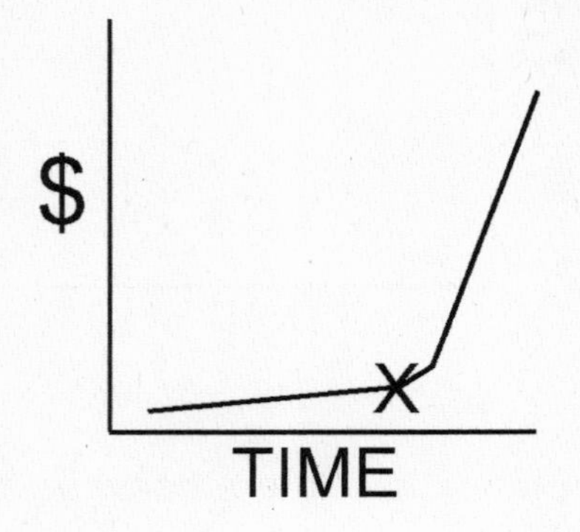

One of the biggest challenges in selling is to get past that X point. That means sticking with your job, gathering enough "no" answers, and building up the momentum you need to start realizing a dramatic increase in income.

Action Item

How many "no" answers do you collect in an average day?

Write the number in your notebook and compare it to the number of "yes" answers you typically receive.

Keep reading to learn how to move beyond . . .

Chapter 14

The Ups and Downs of Selling

LET'S LOOK ONCE AGAIN AT THE CONCEPT OF TIME.

I mentioned earlier in the book that my company has an eight-week selling cycle. Assume that today is the first day of January. If one of our sales reps went out today for an initial appointment, he or she would not be able to count on reaching the fourth stage—that is, the closing or *use* stage—until eight weeks later, which would be March 1.

If, on the other hand, that rep had *no appointments whatsoever* on January 1, he or she would *not* have a sale once March 1 rolled around. That makes sense, doesn't it?

In other words, we can never make up for lost time. If we don't have a sales appointment on January 1, and we go an entire month before initiating this "first-discussion" process with someone, there's going to be a drop in income. We're not going to feel that drop immediately, but we are going to feel it eventually. In my company's case, we're going to notice the sales drop eight weeks after the point at which we stopped making initial contact with people, because our selling cycle is eight weeks.

How is that drop going to manifest itself? Well, what usually happens is a salesperson looks at a paycheck and says, "Hey, all of a sudden there's no income coming in!" But this phenomenon hasn't really happened "all of a sudden." As we just saw, it started happening on the *first day of January*, when we stopped scheduling our initial contacts with new prospects. The problem is, we often don't *notice* the problem on January 1. We notice it on *March 1*, when our income actually takes a nosedive. Then we scurry to catch up, and of course it takes a while to do that.

Too many salespeople experience this stressful up-and-down income pattern. They have a good week here, a bad week there; a good month here, a bad month there; a good quarter here, a bad quarter there. Selling doesn't have to be like that. It really is in our power to even out the seemingly inevitable up-and-down cycle. How, you ask? Read on.

When I train salespeople, I ask them this question: "If you had 100 prospects, would you expect all 100 to close?" Usually, I'll get the right answer, which sounds like this: "No—only a fraction will close." Good salespeople, we find, will typically close about one-fifth of their prospects. (That's in line with the 20:5:1 ratio you learned about in Chapter 13.)

Our experience is that most sales reps are working with no more than twenty prospects at any given time. In most cases, that's all they can physically handle. The problem arises when they fail to *replenish* their prospect base. Intelligent replenishment of prospects is the key to keeping the up-and-down cycle even.

A few years ago, I worked with a salesperson I'll call Mike, whose selling patterns matched the 20:5:1 model. I learned that Mike had, in fact, begun his year with twenty prospects—the typical number. Then he closed a sale. At that point, he thought that he had nineteen prospects left. Did he really?

If we look back at that 20:5:1 ratio, we realize that Mike didn't really have nineteen prospects left. *For every sale he closed, he could count on losing not one, but five total prospects*. After all, that's what the ratio means!

So when Mike closed that first sale of the year, he didn't really have nineteen prospects, although he certainly thought he did. In fact, because he failed to replace the *one* prospect that turned into a sale with *five* new prospects, he was down to fifteen. He just didn't know it yet!

Ignoring his own ratios, Mike pressed ahead. He closed another sale. Once again, he imagined he had plenty of prospects left in his base and concluded that he was a long way away from having to rebuild his prospect base. At this point, the inevitable mathematics of his own ratios should have persuaded him that he was really working with ten live prospects. But he counted (and relied on) eighteen. He made yet another sale and imagined that he had seventeen live prospects left, but the grim reality was that he was down to five. When he made another sale, he imagined that he had sixteen quality prospects left. In fact, *he had zero*.

At that point, Mike sabotaged himself by doing what I've seen countless other salespeople do. He wasted a month trying to sell all his "remaining" prospects and neglected to prospect for any new business. When every single one of these people turned him down—which was what his own numbers would have predicted had Mike taken the trouble to consult them—he panicked. He thought to himself, "Oh, my gosh—I've got no prospects left. I'd better get busy." Then he spent another month building up twenty new prospects so he could start the process all over again. Of course, while he was building up his base, he wasn't closing any new business!

Mike had fallen into the complacency trap. It's a very dangerous cycle that looks like the following graph.

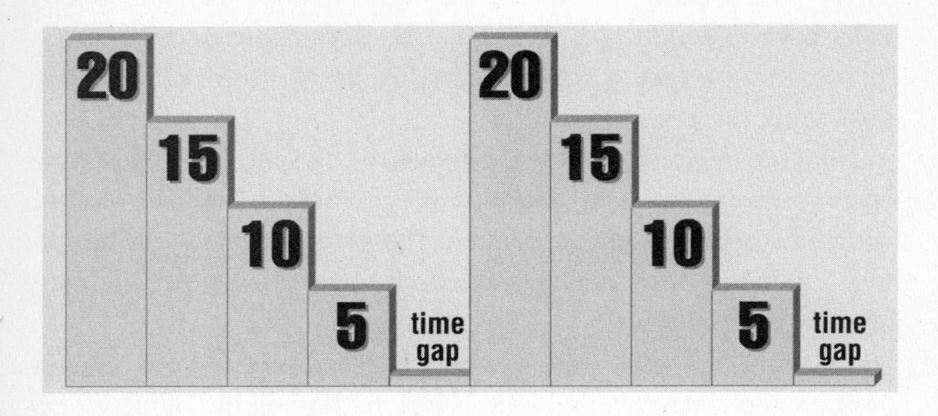

That's the up-and-down cycle so many people fall into. To avoid it, we have to have a *number* of sales coming in consistently. That means new prospects are being developed and mature prospects are closing every week, every month, and every quarter. And we have to maintain our base of prospects at the correct level *at all times.* In order to do that, we cannot simply replace one prospect with another prospect when we close a sale! It's more likely that we're going to have to replenish our base with *five* new prospects.

Mike did a lot better once he mastered the following concept:

$$IC \rightarrow P \rightarrow S$$

That stands for "Initial Contacts yield Prospects, and Prospects yield Sales." The "Initial Contacts" symbol represents our first "good conversation" with a decision-maker. When we make Initial Contact, we talk with someone who *could* decide to do business with us, and we have reason to believe that person could soon turn into a prospect. You remember what that word means: someone who's demonstrated a willingness to play ball with us, typically by engaging in a *second* good discussion of our products and services.

Action Item

Look at your own numbers and review.

How many initial contacts does it typically take for you to develop a single prospect—someone who is still "playing ball" with you on a second or subsequent call? (An Initial Contact is your first good conversation with a decision-maker.) How many prospects do you now have? How many must you *replenish your own base with* whenever you make a sale? (Big hint: The answer is *not* "one.")

Initial Contacts require follow-through on our part in the short term. In other words, someone who tells us "This sounds great–call me next year" does not qualify as an initial contact. Someone who keeps having the same wonderful discussion with us over and over again but won't commit to any future step is no longer an initial contact.

Here's an important distinction to keep in mind. Prospects are people who have *proved to us* that they are interested in following through with a second or subsequent Next Step. Initial contacts are people who, after a single call, *sound like* they're interested in working through the sales process with us. Initial contacts are the promising people we just talked to who have yet to *prove* that they're willing to work through the sales process with us.

Notice that, in the graphic above, the Initial Contact symbol is larger than the Prospects symbol, which in turn is larger than the Sales symbol. That's because not every initial contact will turn into a prospect who continues to "play ball" with us, and not every prospect will turn into a sale!

You're now ready to move on to the next chapter and discover one of the most important principles in all of sales. It's a deceptively simple principle that can and will transform your career once you master it. I'm referring to the principle that . . .

Chapter 15

People Respond in Kind

HAVE YOU EVER PLAYED THAT PARTY GAME TELEPHONE? It goes like this: A message is whispered around the room from person to person. By the end of the game, the initial message has been transformed into a nonsense sentence. That's a little bit like what we're up against when we try to sell to people.

One of our senior trainers, Steve Bookbinder, has a saying: "People barely communicate as it is." Most of the veteran telemarketers I talk to agree with that statement, and even outside salespeople experience the problem Steve is talking about. What salespeople tell their clients is a little different than what they may have meant to say. What their clients hear is a little different than what the salespeople actually said. What the clients remember is different from what they actually heard. And what the clients tell their associates gets changed even further.

By the time this whole process spins itself out, the salesperson's original one-hour presentation gets reduced to the customer saying to somebody else, "I spoke to a salesperson from the XYZ Company yesterday . . . or was it the ABC Company? Anyway they had right-handed widgets . . . or was it left-handed widgets?"

This is a bit of an exaggeration, of course, but Steve is definitely right: People barely communicate. And over the phone, of course, there's even less communication. For one thing, the actual phone transmission can make it difficult to hear what the other person is saying. (Anyone who's ever held a conversation involving a cellular phone can attest to this.) For another thing, we have no access to visual signals when we're talking on the phone. But what *really* blocks people's ability to hear what we're saying is our own ignorance of what the other person is trying to do!

If we stray from what's interesting to a prospect into an area that's *not* interesting, our conversation is in trouble. Our message is going to get distorted. We have an obligation, as telesales professionals, to keep the conversation interesting. And what is most interesting to the people we're calling? What they do! It's a law as reliable as the law of gravity: *People are most interested in what they themselves are doing, how they do it, and why they do it.* Therefore, to move forward in the conversation and the relationship, we must constantly focus on what the people we're calling are doing, what they're trying to accomplish, and what they want to make happen.

This means we're going to ask them questions about what they're doing, how they're doing it, and why they're doing it. However, we have to understand that when we get on the phone, we can't simply begin the conversation with a barrage of questions. Imagine how you'd feel if you were walking from one place to another in your office, and you ran into a total stranger in the hall, and that person suddenly cornered you and started asking a series of questions. You'd get a little upset by that because you wouldn't have any idea who on earth you were talking to!

To avoid such problems, we need to be mindful of some governing principles that can help us figure out what's interesting to the other person during a phone conversation. First and foremost is this reliable proposition: People tend to respond in kind to what we say and how we say it.

Let me give you an example. Suppose you picked up the telephone at work and heard me say, very politely, "Good morning, this is Steve Schiffman. May I ask who I'm speaking with?" You'd probably tell me your name.

What if, on the other hand, I called you up and said, very brusquely, "Who is this?" You would give me a very different response indeed. You'd probably take the structure of my question—and its unprofessional tone—and turn it right back in my direction by asking, "Who is *this?*" Certainly you'd feel less inclined to give me your name.

Why does that difference exist when I'm asking for the same thing in both situations? The answer is that *you're responding in kind to both the structure and the tone of my question.* If I'm helpful, if I'm open, if I'm honest, if I'm professional, you'll tend to respond in the same way. On the other hand, if I'm abrasive, if I'm curt, if I'm aggressive, if I'm confrontational, you'll tend to give me a response that matches those patterns.

I repeat: People really do respond in kind to what we say and how we say it. Once we realize that, we can position ourselves effectively to learn what we need to learn about what other people *do.*

I mentioned earlier that focusing on "what the prospect needs" is a potentially fatal mistake. Like many of the salespeople we train, you may have been skeptical about that statement. Consider, though, if you call someone up, introduce yourself pleasantly, and then ask, "What do you need this quarter in terms of inventory software?" what kind of answer are you likely to get? You can probably hear it already: "I don't need anything. Good-bye!" They've responded in kind to the structure of your question!

Suppose, though, you called the same person, introduced yourself, established a little rapport, and asked, "What are you *doing* right now to manage your inventory?" You'd get a totally different response, wouldn't you? You might even get an answer that encouraged the person to open up and give you some information.

People really do respond in kind to us. Do you realize what that means? That means we can affect what happens in the conversation by carefully selecting the questions we ask. This is a vitally important principle, one that will become more clear to you as you move forward in this book.

Action Item

Write down three questions that would encourage the other person to respond with an initial response like "I'm not interested." Then try to rewrite the questions in such a way as to focus on *what the person does* or is trying to accomplish in a given area.

In the next chapter, you'll learn about another vitally important principle for sales success, namely . . .

Chapter 16

Interruptive Marketing

WHAT WOULD HAPPEN IF I were to walk into your work area unannounced and ask, "Where did you get those shoes? What about that shirt? What about that belt?" How many questions would I be able to ask before you finally gave up and said something like, "Hey, let me ask *you* a question: Who the heck are you and why are you asking me all these questions?"

Now suppose that I walk into your work area, introduce myself cordially, shake your hand, and say, "Listen, I bought a belt like that down the street about six years ago, but the store went out of business and now I can't seem to find anything like it. Can I ask you where you got that belt?"

It's much easier to give me the information in that scenario, isn't it? I could quickly find out where you bought the belt, and I could even repeat the process for the shirt, the shoes, or just about anything else I wanted to learn.

Here's why: Every time I *tell* you something about me, I have won the right to *ask* a question about you. That's my opportunity to learn more about what you do. I could do this by saying, "You know, we find that a lot of the companies we work with do so-and-so. Just out of curiosity, how do you handle that issue at your company?" This is *interruptive marketing*—revealing something about ourselves and using that fact to refocus the conversation with a new question.

This approach is extremely effective, as is the concept of structuring your questions around the idea that people will respond in kind to what you say over the phone. I'm sharing these two vitally important ideas with you now because I want you to be ready to ask the right questions the instant the opportunity presents itself. Once you get past Critical Point #1—and you'll learn how to do that in the following chapters—you'll want to keep an eye open for every opportunity to gather information.

For instance, if you were selling telephone and communication services, you'd want to know:

Who is the current carrier?
How long has this company been with that carrier?
How and why did the company choose that carrier?*
Who else is the decision-maker looking at now?
Who has the decision-maker looked at in the past?
Why didn't those carriers make sense?
How many people use long distance as a regular part of the job?
Who are the company's principal customers?
How do customers get in touch with the company?
Who are the most important competitors?

---

* *(Important note: If your contact has no idea how the purchase decision was made in the past or what the criteria are for making the purchase in the future, that's a sign that you are not dealing with the true decision-maker. In virtually all cases, you are much better off asking "How did you decide on XYZ company?" than you are asking "Are you the decision-maker?" The answer will demonstrate clearly how much your contact knows . . . and who has ultimate decision-making authority.)*

What competitive challenges does the company face in the near future?

Who are the company's most important suppliers?

How many sales reps, field service people, and other "on the road" people does the company employ?

How do people at the central office keep in touch with those who work outside the office?

And so on. When we get to the interview step, we're going to use this "my turn to ask" principle, as well as the principle you learned in Chapter 15 about people responding in kind, to gather information that will help you figure out exactly what's interesting *to the other person.* Specifically, we're going to respond to the question or issue that the other person raises with us and then take advantage of the fact that, by doing so, we've won the right to ask a question of our own.

Please keep in mind that these ideas are tools you can use to improve your conversation. They're not ironclad rules you must try to apply to every question that comes out of your mouth.

By the way, in addition to asking questions about the company like the ones you just read, you're also going to try to find out the most important information about the *person* you're talking to. For instance:

What does this person do?

How did this person win a job with this company?

How long has he or she worked for this company?

Roughly how old is this person, and how long has he or she been doing this particular job?

What does this person see on the career horizon?

Notice that each of these questions ties into the "DO." By asking prospects about what they *do, have done, and plan to do*, we're going to find out not only about activity, but also about the *language* people use to describe what's happening in their company and in their careers. That's going to be crucial, because when we start to use the prospect's own language to explain how our products and services work, that's going to go help the prospect to visualize exactly what we're talking about.

Action Item

In your notebook, please write down the following: ONCE I RESPOND TO YOUR QUESTION OR ISSUE AND TELL YOU SOMETHING ABOUT ME, I HAVE WON THE RIGHT TO ASK YOU A QUESTION ABOUT WHAT *YOU* DO.

The two principles you've read about in this chapter and Chapter 15 are vitally important. I've shared them with you at this relatively early point in the book because you really can't conduct the second, or information-gathering, step without them. Please be sure you familiarize yourself with these two ideas *before* you map out your calling script. Once you are thoroughly familiar with this material, keep reading to find out . . .

Chapter 17

Why Writing It All Down Is Essential

VERY SOON, YOU'LL START WORK on your own customized telesales script—or, as we prefer to call it, your approach. I realize that your initial reaction to the idea of formalizing words on paper in this way may be negative: "I hate scripts! They make you sound so stiff. They are the opposite of that free-flowing conversation that I really want to have." Well, the good news is that your call doesn't have to sound unnatural at all.

Movies have scripts, don't they? Yet the best movies don't sound in the least stilted. Why? Because the actors practice the script over and over again until the words become second nature. Well, we can practice our approach, too, and we can do something that actors usually *can't* do. We can develop our material ourselves, choosing a style that's unique to us. We can make what we say very conversational. As a matter of fact, we can make our interactions *more* relaxed and natural-sounding than we can if we weren't trying to formalize our approach. Let me explain what I mean.

Putting the words down on paper ahead of time means that you take the time when you're *not* on the phone with a person to develop a concise way of saying what you want to say when you *are* on the phone. Now, this isn't a magic incantation that instantly turns skeptical contacts into instant prospects. On the contrary, your approach will serve one and only one function: It will elicit a response from the person you're calling. As we've seen, that response will almost certainly be negative. It's Critical Point #1. You're going to say something, and the other person is going to say, "Wait a minute. I'm not interested. I don't have time for this. I've already got something like this."

So why do we want to have all the words down ahead of time? Because that first response is like a ball that's thrown at you at 90 miles an hour. For you to properly catch that ball and throw it back—for you to turn that objection around—you're going to have to hear it and identify it accurately in just a split second. And unfortunately, if you're busy thinking about what *you're* going to say, you're going to miss what *the other person* just said. You need to formalize your approach so you're not wasting time or mental energy thinking about what you're going to say next.

Once you master your words—and please understand that these are *your* words, not anyone else's—you can focus on listening to what the other person is saying *regardless of who's actually talking*. You're using an approach that you've internalized so many times that you don't even have to think about it. You don't have to hear yourself say any of the words. You're able to react quickly and accurately to the issue that's hurtling your way at 90 miles per hour.

I realize that the idea of "using a script" for your calls may be something new and different to you, just like a lot of the ideas in this book may sound new or different. Remember my story about the golf grip! Positive changes in our routine *usually* feel uncomfortable at first. Bear that in mind as you move through the next chapters.

Understand, too, that the aim of finalizing an approach is *not* to "handcuff" you or to lay out a blueprint of your entire conversation with the other person. Instead, you want to script out the *first few seconds* of the conversation in order to *get the first negative response out on the table* so you can identify it and turn it around.

Action Item

In your notebook and in your own words, write at least three reasons it is in your best interest as a sales professional to formalize your calling approach.

Keep reading to find out how the formal calling approach you eventually develop and internalize will help you to . . .

Chapter 18

Master the Game of Catch

HAVE YOU NOTICED? Every year in sales, the competition gets stronger, the territory gets harder to work, and our goals go up. It stands to reason, then, that if we're still doing exactly the same things in exactly the same way we did them last year, the best we can hope to achieve is last year's results. In sales, however, last year's results usually don't cut it this year. That's why we're constantly asked to reevaluate, to identify what's working and what isn't, and to change those things that are not working. And that's precisely what you're getting ready to do in this part of the book.

We've been building up for quite some time to the work you're about to begin in earnest in Chapter 19. Because our company has trained thousands upon thousands of telemarketers, I know full well that what I'm about to ask you to do may seem new and different and uncomfortable. All the same, it's very, very important that you do it anyway—because it's only by adopting proven techniques that you can really bring about positive changes in your selling routine.

At various points in this book, I've compared the selling process to the act of "playing ball." And that's an image I want you to keep in mind as you start building your script. If you throw a ball back and forth with someone, you see some interesting parallels with selling. For instance: I surprise you by throwing a ball your way, and yet for some reason your instincts take over and you're able to catch it. Why?

Most of us can answer that question by looking back at our own childhood. When you were, say, two years old, there came a time at the beach or in the backyard when someone threw a great big ball your way. My guess is that no matter how that person tried to prepare you for what was about to happen, the ball fell right through your hands—if it got near your hands at all. By the time you were six or so, you were able to catch the ball, but only by paying very close attention and wrapping your arms around it entirely when it came your way. Today, as a grown-up, your experience is probably like mine; someone suddenly tosses a tennis ball your way, and just before it arrives, you make the necessary physical adjustment and catch the ball without any problem. What's the difference between the performance of the two-year-old and the six-year-old? Practice and experience. What's the difference between the performance of the six-year-old and the adult? Practice and experience.

What does all this have to do with your calling approach—what most salespeople call a script? Well, just like a game of catch, things in sales happen over and over and over again. You've probably played catch a thousand times in your life. If I threw you a ball right now, a little mental file labeled "playing catch" would instantly open up. Amazing, isn't it? You wouldn't know exactly when or how I planned to throw the ball, but once I threw it to you, that mental file would open up, and you would know exactly what to do when the ball reached you.

Here's the point: That ball represents everything that is likely to come up during a sales call. You don't know when it's going to happen or how it's going to happen, but when it does happen, it's just like in catch—you need to know exactly what to do.

Our experience and our practice in playing catch tells us where the ball is liable to land. With our experience in sales, we know just the kinds of things people are likely to say to us. Questions, issues, concerns, objections, and situations take place in roughly the same way, time and time again. We really have heard it all before. In sales, there are really no surprises. And yet, some salespeople act surprised each time they encounter these similar situations. As a result, they waste a lot of time and energy trying to come up with a new way to deal with an old problem.

That's wrong. There's no reason to make up a new "best answer" every single time someone tells you, "I have no interest whatsoever." What we need to do instead is perfect the right turnaround, memorize it, and then throw the ball back.

But that ball is traveling back and forth at 90 miles an hour, so our approach is basically a tool for initiating a verbal game of catch, and a very fast one at that. It's going to help us get the initial objection out on the table so we can move on to ask questions that will make the conversation interesting to the prospect. Remember, if we can't get past that initial response—which is Critical Point #1—we have nothing! On the other hand, if we do turn around that initial response we've heard hundreds or thousands or maybe even tens of thousands of times, then we can launch an extended conversation. And that's very good; that's what we want, because, as we've seen, our first "good call" with someone is known as the Initial Contact, and that's what drives our sales activity. Remember the following formula.

$IC_{\rightarrow P_{\rightarrow S}}$

Initial Contacts lead to Prospects, and Prospects Lead to Sales!

Action Item

Describe your ideal sales call.

Briefly write down the dialogue of your ideal sales call in your notebook. Take ten to fifteen minutes to develop the lines you would hear in an *ideal* two-way conversation between yourself and a decision-maker. (*Note:* This is not your calling approach; it's an exercise to help you identify what you want out of the first few seconds of the call.)

If you've made it this far . . . if you've read every chapter in full . . . if you've completed all the Action Items . . . you're now ready to begin Chapter 19. It's one of the most important chapters in the whole book because it represents the point where you begin . . .

Chapter 19

Developing Your Attention Statement

LET'S START TO BUILD YOUR CALLING APPROACH.

The first thing we want to do when we make a phone call is get the other person's attention. In the old days, telephone salespeople solved this problem by saying "salesy" things like, "Mr. Smith, if I could earn you a million dollars in the stock market in thirty days, would you do business with me today?" Or: "Mr. Smith, do you want to stop losing your best people to the competition?" Or: "Mr. Smith, if I could cut your bills by 25 percent, would you work with me?" Or: "Mr. Smith, if your current supplier suddenly went bankrupt, you'd be in big trouble, wouldn't you?"

In today's world those openings don't help you much. People automatically tune them out. Don't believe me? Think back to the last call you received from a telemarketer who used an opening like this. Ask yourself whether the opening the person used actually led to an extended, information-rich conversation.

Despite the fact that those techniques actually stopped working at least twenty years ago, the sad truth is they're still used today. To succeed at the highest level today, we have to take a much more conversational, much more professional approach, an approach that's both honest and direct. One reason we have to do this is that this approach simply works best. Another reason we need to be honest and direct is that we have to work against the bad reputation that's been built up over the years by virtually every other telemarketer who's ever talked to the person we're calling.

All those telephone salespeople your contact has dealt with over the years have been evasive, misleading, and downright dishonest. They've lied about the reason for their call, the company they work for, or the details of their product/service offering. And telemarketers are still doing all this today!

That means we have to make it absolutely clear from the very first second of our call that we are not going to conduct the conversation that way. We have to bend over backwards to be simple, direct, honest, and forthcoming, since bad experience has made the people we're calling suspicious when they pick up the phone. So what's the best way to get someone's attention in today's world? It's simply to use the person's name:

"Hi–Joe Jones?"

or:

"Good morning, Mr. Jones."

It's honest, and it works! The very best way to get somebody's attention is simply to say the person's name; so steer clear of the gimmicks and begin using your contact's name.

By the way, although you can use whatever approach is comfortable for you and regionally appropriate, many top salespeople avoid calling people "Mr." or "Mrs." They see themselves as one professional calling another professional, and they feel that those titles can put up artificial barriers between people. On the other hand, if the person's name is Jim, and I call up and say, "Good morning, Jim," despite the fact that we're total strangers at that moment, Jim may find that approach overly familiar. So a good approach is simply to use both names: "Good morning–Joe Jones?"

That's my preference, but you should use whatever you're comfortable with. Just be sure you build your opening–which is technically known as the Attention Statement–around the person's name and nothing else.

Action Item

In your notebook, compose an initial draft of your Attention Statement.

Keep reading to begin . . .

Chapter 20

Developing Your Identification Statement

THE SECOND THING YOU HAVE TO DO DURING THE CALL is identify who you are and who your company is. If you work at a giant, well-known company, a company that is in the *Fortune* 500, for example, the chances are good that when you mention who you are and the company's name, people will be familiar with it. However, if you work at a company that is not well known, you'll have to say just a little more to build up your credibility.

This identification piece is a vitally important step that most telesales salespeople skip. That's an unfortunate omission. Have you ever called someone you wanted to sell to and fifteen or twenty seconds into the call, the person on the other end of the line stops you in midsentence and says, "Excuse me, who is this? Where are you from?" It's not easy to come back from that exchange.

What we may forget is that the person on the other end of the phone needs to have a moment to synchronize his or her hearing process with your speaking process. If you speak faster than the other person is accustomed to listening, it's going to take a moment for him or her to adjust to your rate of speech. If your accent or dialect is unfamiliar, the other person will need a moment to adjust to that. The Identification Step gives the person you're calling that opportunity. It serves as a kind of buffer and gives the person you're talking to a chance to catch up with you.

Your Identification Statement should sound something like this:

> *"This is Steve Schiffman calling from D.E.I. Management Group. I don't know whether or not you've heard of us, but we're one of the largest sales training organizations in the country. We've worked with companies like A, B, C, and D."*

or:

> *"This is Mike Miller, calling from the Boston office of Huge Corporation."*

Take a moment now to build your Identification Statement. Use words that are comfortable and natural to you, but make sure that your Identification Statement accomplishes the same things the samples you've just read accomplish. It should be concise, give your listener a chance to catch up with you and get in synch with the conversation, and provide enough identifying information to answer the question "Who is this?"

Action Item

Compose an initial draft of your Identification Statement.

Do this in your notebook. *Say your Attention Statement and your Identification Statement out loud at least ten times.*

Keep reading to find out about . . .

Chapter 21

Developing the Reason for the Call

THE NEXT THING TO DO is give the person you're calling a reason for the call you're making.

What you're about to read is the basic, plain-vanilla version of this vitally important part of the call. A little later, in Chapter 29, you'll learn how to put together a couple of very effective refinements on the basic version. What follows is the simplest approach; everything else is an enhancement on this.

Let's look at some core principles. When people receive a call from a person who is unfamiliar to them, they tend to have two reactions. The first reaction is a question. People ask themselves, "Should I be getting this call?" In other words, people want to find out whether this call is really for them at all. They ask themselves whether they can pass the call off to someone else or, even better, disengage from it and ignore it entirely.

The second thing that happens—and it usually happens the very instant that people have answered that "Should I be getting this call?" question in the affirmative—also takes the form of a question. People ask themselves, "What's in this for me?" They want to know what they're going to get out of the exchange—why they should keep listening. Put concisely, they want us to tell them the answer to the question, "So what?"

Those are tough questions, and we have to address them directly. After you get the person's attention and identify yourself, you have to deal with both of those issues. The first thing you have to do is say what the call is all about, and the second thing you have to do is answer the question "What's in it for me?"

Obviously, this second component is a crucial part of your approach. You should spend a fair amount of time drafting it. Your reason for the call should follow this sequence: "The reason I'm calling you today specifically is to tell you about such-and-such a feature that could benefit you in this specific way." *Notice that we address the "Is this my call?" question in the first part and the "What's in it for me?" question in the second part.*

Here's what it might sound like in action:

(Silent question: "Is this my call?") *"The reason I'm calling you today specifically is to tell you about . . ."*

(Silent question: "What's in it for me?") *". . . our cold-calling programs, which can help your people make more appointments."*

Or:

(Silent question: "Is this my call?") *"The reason I'm calling you today specifically is to tell you about . . ."*

(Silent question: "What's in it for me?") *". . . a program we offer that can dramatically improve the mileage you get from your company's fleet of trucks."*

Remember: The main reason to write these words down and

practice them is to elicit a response from the other person. At some point, the person you're talking to will respond, and generating that response is the whole point of formalizing your approach. So don't misunderstand. This is not a magic incantation. The game of telesales doesn't begin when you say hello. It begins when the other person gives you a response. And so far, we've got a great outline for eliciting that response. Take a look at it again:

- *Attention Statement*
- *Identification Statement*
- *Reason for the Call*

(By the way, if you're selling in an inbound telesales environment, you'll find a variation designed for your situation in Chapter 29.)

Build up your approach, and remember as you do so that the whole point of what you're doing is to get interrupted, to get the response, to get to Critical Point #1.

Action Item

Compose an initial draft of your Reason for the Call. *Say your Attention Statement, your Identification Statement, and your Reason for the Call out loud at least ten times.*

Keep reading to find out . . .

Chapter 22

What to Do If You Don't Get Interrupted

THIS IS ONE OF THE SIMPLEST CHAPTERS in the book.

If you somehow make it all the way through the first three components of your script or approach without hearing a negative response like "We're not interested" or "I'm too busy to deal with this right now," your job is simple. You're going to ask a question and elicit a response from the other person. Don't ask permission to ask a question. Simply ask a question.

Assume (for the sake of argument) that you're selling telecommunications services. Look once again at the long list of things you'd like to be able to find out about the organization and the person you're calling.

Who is the current carrier?
How long has this company been with that carrier?
How and why did the company choose that carrier?
Who else is the decision-maker looking at now?

Who has the decision-maker looked at in the past?
Why didn't those carriers make sense?
How many people use long distance as a regular part of the job?
Who are the company's principal customers?
How do customers get in touch with the company?
Who are the most important competitors?
What competitive challenges does the company face in the near future?
Who are the company's most important suppliers?
How many sales reps, field service people, and other "on the road" people does the company employ?
How do people at the central office keep in touch with those who work outside the office?
What does this person do?
How did this person win a job with this company?
How long has he or she worked for this company?
Roughly how old is this person?
What does this person see on the career horizon?

There's certainly a lot of ground to cover! In the unlikely (but not unheard-of) event that your contact gives you no negative response, you can assume for the moment that you have sailed past Critical Point #1 and attempt to move directly into the second, information-gathering step. You probably *haven't* made it around Critical Point #1 which is why you'll want to read Chapters 24 through 28 carefully, but you should nevertheless *prepare and practice your first question ahead of time.*

In the absence of a negative first response to turn around, you might choose to ask one of the following questions:

- I'm just curious—who are you using now?

- I'm just curious—how did you choose your current carrier? (Again, asking this question or some variation on it is the *very best* way to identify a decision-maker.)
- I'm just curious—how do your customers get in touch with you right now?

Those are all good first questions, but my favorite question—and the one I recommend to everyone I train—is much more effective and much more direct. It takes a little practice and a little courage, but it's well worth the effort. It sounds like this:

- I was looking at my records, and I noticed that you're not using us. I was just curious—why not?

I promise you that you will be *amazed* at the information you will uncover when you ask this question and wait confidently for the answer. The ultimate goal of your conversation is to launch the first "good call"—the Initial Contact that marks the beginning of

Action Item

Develop two questions you can use to get a response at the outset of the call.

Write each in your notebook. Be sure one of the questions is a variation on "Why aren't you working with us now?" *Practice saying each question out loud at least ten times.*

the sales process in the telesales environment. I have come across no better way to initiate that call than by using some version of the question you just read to enter the second, information-gathering step of the sale.

The point of your initial calling approach is to *elicit an initial response*. That response is likely to be negative, and it's likely to sound very imposing. Keep reading to find out why . . . as we take a short detour to . . .

Chapter 23

The Department Store

IN MOST CASES, OF COURSE, YOU *WILL* BE INTERRUPTED by the person you've called. When that happens, you'll be at Critical Point #1. What you will hear from the other person at that point will sound valid and perhaps even difficult to overcome.

You'll develop specific turnarounds for all the response groups a little later in the book. For right now, though, I want you to understand that the *first* reason the person gives you almost always sounds more difficult to manage than it really is. This is an extremely important point. More often than you imagine, that first response you hear really *can* be turned around . . . if only you prepare yourself for it properly.

Consider this scenario. You're in a department store. You're walking down the aisle. You're looking at merchandise. You're considering making a purchase. All of a sudden, a salesperson comes up to you and asks, "Can I help you?" How do you respond?

Most of us respond quickly and instinctively by saying, "No, no. I'm just looking." So what happens next? The salesperson turns around and walks away. But before the person vanishes, we often reconsider and say, "Oh, wait a minute. There is that one thing. Where are the sneakers?" If you're like me, you've had that very experience more than once.

Here's my question. What's behind that initial "just looking" response?

Well, the instant the salesperson approaches us, we've somehow been programmed to say something that basically translates as, "Salesperson, go away." It's just a universal response. And as imposing as it may sound, I don't even think it's really voluntary.

Do you realize what that means? It means that everywhere in the world, every salesperson in every industry in every country gets that superficial, knee-jerk, valid-sounding response that *sounds* like an objection. And yet, very often we find that customers who eventually buy from us started out in exactly the same way. They initially said, "I'm not interested," or "I'm very busy," or "I'm happy with what I have now." And even though those responses seemed impossible to turn around at the time, people ended up buying from us.

Let's do a little exercise now. Put a check mark by each of the following initial responses that you personally have heard from people you called.

I'm not interested.
I've already got it.
We're using your competitor.
I have no time.
I have no money.
We once had a problem with your company.
We don't need it.

It just doesn't fit in.

We don't have the budget for it.

Do those sound familiar? They should. Now place a check mark next to each of the questions below that you've heard during sales calls:

Gee, how much is it?

Can you mail me some literature?

Before you go on, why should I switch to you?

What makes your company so good?

(When you know nothing whatsoever about the prospect:) Take it from the top—tell me everything, okay?

Can't you just give me the thirty-second version of your presentation?

Did these questions seem familiar to you, as well? Of course they did. Can you guess why? Every salesperson gets the same list of so-called "objections" (we prefer to call them "issues") at the outset of the call. What's more, every salesperson hears the same kinds of seemingly impossible questions.

What does this tell us? It tells us that the responses we hear at Critical Point #1 are not as valid as they seem. Remember: Whenever you're in a department store, whenever you see that little "I'm just looking" drama played out, what you're actually seeing is a very simple model of what happens to all salespeople every time they attempt to engage a perspective customer in any kind of a conversation. People throw up roadblocks instinctively, and they tend to do so in predictable ways.

Since we work with so many salespeople in so many selling environments, we have the chance to see this phenomenon take place universally, across all industry lines. The initial response to any salesperson's attempt to engage us in a conversation is always some predictable variation on "Salesperson, go away. I don't need a salesperson." But there's very often a little voice that's just waiting for a chance to say, "Wait a minute—where are the socks, anyway?"

Think about it. When you call someone who instantly says "I can't afford it," what does that really mean? Does it mean that that company has investigated your fee structure, compared it to their cash flow, and determined scientifically that their organization can't afford to work with you for the first and second quarters of this year? Or is the person instead indulging a knee-jerk reaction that's very similar to the person in the department store who says "No, no. I'm just looking"?

We have a script, and so do the people we call. In fact, once you turn around that first response, you'll often find that you get a different second response, one that's a little closer to the actual issue the person is facing. That's because *the longer the conversation goes on, and the better our connection with the person we're calling, the more reliable the information tends to be.*

Action Item

If you haven't already done so, write in your notebook the ten most common negative responses you hear over the phone.

Are you ready for a surprise? All of the initial negative responses we hear—including every one you just wrote in your notebook—can be grouped into one of just four main categories.

That's right: Every single negative response you hear over the phone can be assigned, for the purpose of the turnaround, into one of just four categories. We saw before that the purpose of a script is to allow you to get the response out on the table and hear it clearly. In the next chapter, you'll start to learn about the categories you'll be listening for—and what to do when you hear one.

So begin now by learning about the first kind of initial negative response, which is . . .

Chapter 24

"Happy Now"

THE FIRST NEGATIVE RESPONSE CATEGORY is one we call "Happy Now." Salespeople get this quite a lot over the phone. The response can take many forms, but it tends to sound like this:

We are happy now—all set.
We're doing it ourselves.
We just signed a contract yesterday.
We're doing it in-house.
We're working with your competition.
We're all set.
We don't need anything else because we've already got exactly what you sell.

Here's a story that will show you how to turn this seemingly difficult objection around. Steve Bookbinder called a large property and casualty insurance company a while ago. He was trying to figure out who within the organization handled sales training. All the fingers pointed to a gentleman by the name of Fred, whose title was Senior Vice President of Marketing. The problem was that Fred was very difficult to reach. You could only reach Fred if you called him at precisely 7:00 in the morning–not 6:55, mind you, and not 7:05, but 7:00 on the dot. So Steve Bookbinder made his way to the office by 6:45 so that he would be ready to call Fred at 7:00 sharp. At 6:59, Steve got his pad and pen ready. At 6:59 and thirty seconds, he started to dial the number slowly. At 7:00 exactly, Fred's direct line rang. Fred picked up the phone and said, "Fred."

Steve said, "Fred Jones? Hi. This is Steve Bookbinder. I'm with D.E.I. Management Group. We're a sales training company in New York; I don't know whether or not you've heard of us, but–"

That's as far as he got. Fred broke in and said, "Steve, your timing stinks. Let me just tell you something. We've already figured out that we need sales training, and in fact I put this job out to bid over a month ago. I asked the biggest training companies in America to bid on the project. I'm sorry we didn't ask you, but that's the way it goes. Just the other day I selected the company we're going to go with. I not only selected the training vendor, but I selected the training programs, the training material, the training site, and the training location. I've identified all of the training participants, so guess what? We're all set. We're as set as set can get. You're too late. Your timing just stinks."

Steve had to listen to that at seven o'clock in the morning! How do you think he felt?

Actually, he was pretty happy. He had just learned that Fred was in fact the person in charge of buying sales training. That's good, because we sell sales training, so there was a match!

So what did Steve do next? Well, he could have said, "I guess

I missed it this year; you're right, Fred. I'm just curious, when are you going to buy next year's training?" The purpose of his call, however, was to engage Fred in a sales conversation then and there. So that wouldn't have worked.

Or Steve could have asked, "Fred, who did you actually end up going with?" In some situations, that would have been a great question, but Steve chose against it at this point in the call because he didn't want Fred to assume that the call was about to become confrontational. ("Oh, you chose XYZ? Gee, that's too bad—because we're much better.") The point was not to convince Fred that he'd made a poor decision, but to engage Fred in the kind of "good first call" dialogue that results in a scheduled first appointment—or, in a telesales environment, what we call Initial Contact. Steve asked himself, How can I make that happen?

Here's what Steve said to Fred:

"Fred, do you know what? Other companies in your business have told me the same thing. They were also working with other training companies before they saw how we could complement what they were doing. I'd like to get together and show you how. How's Tuesday at three?"

Guess what happened next? Fred said, "Okay. Tuesday at three sounds fine."

Look at it again. Steve said to him, "Other people have said the same thing before they saw how we can complement what they're already doing." And if he didn't like the word complement, he could have used enhance, match, fits into, adds to, contributes to. In other words, whatever Fred is doing now is fine. We could just make it work better. We've done that for lots of companies who initially told us they were "all set," and I'm sure that, if you think about your company's customers, you'll realize that the same is true in your selling environment.

For now, don't worry about how you'll continue the telesales conversation once you've turned around the "Happy Now" response. Just familiarize yourself with the following key principle:

When you hear a "Happy Now" response, turn it around with COMPLEMENT/MATCH/FIT.

Example: You know, other companies we do business with told us exactly the same thing before they saw how what we offered could complement what they were already doing.

Action Item

Write down your own version of the COMPLEMENT/MATCH/FIT turnaround in your notebook. *Practice it out loud at least ten times.*

Keep reading to find out how to turn around the next initial negative response, which is . . .

Chapter 25

"Not Interested"

THE NEXT RESPONSE CATEGORY is known as the "Not Interested" category. This one has a great many variations. Here are some of them:

We have absolutely no interest whatsoever.
We have no reason to buy that right now.
It's not in the plan.
We had a bad experience with you in the past.
I have no time to deal with this.
We have no money.
That's not a priority.
The president has decided against this.
We don't do that.
We hate you.

All of these are examples of different versions of the "Not Interested" negative response.

We encountered that response not long ago when we called one of the largest accounting firms in the country. Here's the response that came back to our rep about four seconds into the call: "We're not salespeople here. We have absolutely no interest in sales training. We don't sell here, okay? We account here. You're wasting your time."

At that point, we shrewdly recognized that we had reached Critical Point #1 and that we had encountered a "Not Interested" response.

So what did we do? Did we give up? Did we say, "Not interested, eh? That's a new one. Okay, thanks for your time, and have a great day." No! We said something very different. Here's what it sounded like:

> *"You know what? The last accounting firm we worked with, ABC Accounting, said the exact same thing to us. They initially told us they had no interest in our sales training, but that was before they saw how our training could benefit them by improving their bottom line and increasing the average value of their accounts. We'd like to show you the program we put together for them. How's Tuesday at three?"*

We got the appointment and, eventually, the business.

Look at it again. To turn around "Not interested," we said, "Other people said the same thing before they saw how we could benefit them."

You can use that same turnaround outline in any of the circumstances that fall into the "Not Interested" category. For example, someone may say to you, "Look, I have no time for this." Here's how you can turn it around: "You know, a lot of the people I talk to react that way at first, before they see how we can benefit them." Or suppose someone says, "We have no money." Here's how you can turn it around: "You know, a lot of people tell me that before they see how our products and services can really benefit them."

Suppose someone tells you, "Listen, this is nothing personal, but we once had a problem with your company, and unfortunately for you, we now hate you." Here's the turnaround: "You know, others said that before they saw how we've changed."

Please understand that this is not an argument we're starting but a conversation. We want to reassure the people we're talking to. It's okay that they have that particular response. The response they just gave us doesn't disqualify us from talking. In fact, a lot of people react that way.

Look at it once again: "Many of the people I talk to say the same thing that you're saying to me right now, before they see how we could benefit them." And the benefit around which this turnaround is built answers the question "So what?" or the question "What's in it for me?"

When you hear a "Not Interested" response, turn it around with a BENEFIT.

Example: You know, other companies told me exactly the same thing before they saw how what we offered could benefit them (in such-and-such a way).

Action Item

Write down your own version of the BENEFIT turn-around.

Remember that the *benefit* around which this turn-around is built answers the question "So what?" or the question "What's in it for me?" *Practice this turn-around out loud at least ten times.*

Keep reading to find out how to turn around the next initial negative response, which is . . .

Chapter 26

"Send Literature"

IN A TELESALES SITUATION, people may say to us, "Could you please send me some literature?" That's very different from what happens when an outside salesperson—that is, someone who is seeking a face-to-face appointment—gets the same request. The outside salesperson is asking for an appointment, and in all likelihood "Please send me literature" simply means, "Hey, I don't want to play ball with you."

But when a telesales professional hears "Send me literature," there's a greater chance that that request will fit right into what we want. Why? Because most sales calls that do not result in a one-call close do incorporate some follow-up step that involves sending some kind of material.

There are some problems to consider, though. What literature are we going to send? And why exactly are we sending it? More to the point, what's happening next in the relationship? You'll recall that the objective of the first step of the sales process is to get to the Next Step. That's exactly what we're trying to do here, move from the opening to the information-gathering step. So we need to use that request for literature as a way to get to our next conversation. We can't just roll over and say, "Sure, I'll send the information," and end the call.

In fact, a request for information is potentially quite dangerous, because it can cause us to lose control of the conversation. We must lead the conversation. We're going to do that not by talking the person to death, but by anticipating where we want the call to go next and asking an appropriate question that will get us there.

Here's how to regain control. The prospect says, "Listen, can you please send me some information about this?" And without missing a beat, you're going to say . . .

> *Of course, but I'm just curious— what are you doing right now to reconfigure your widgets?*

In other words, you're going to briefly answer the question and respond with a question of your own about what the person is doing.

Notice that by responding to the person's question, you have won the right to ask a question of your own. By refocusing the conversation on a "do-based" question, you're going to increase the likelihood of having a good, extended conversation—an Initial Contact—with the person you've called. This is a very important technique, one that we originated at my company. We call this selling technique the "Ledge" because it gives you a foothold.

You'll find out a lot more about the Ledge in the next chapter. Before you go on, though, look at it again as it applies to the request for literature.

When you hear a "Send Literature" response, turn it around

with the LEDGE—briefly answer the question and immediately pose a question of your own.

Example: (Can you send me some literature?) Of course. I'm just curious, though, how are you training your salespeople right now?

Action Item

Write down your own version of the turnaround you would use to handle a "Send Literature" response. Respond briefly to the question and pose a question of your own. *Practice this turnaround out loud at least ten times.*

Keep reading to find out how to turn around the next initial negative response, which is . . .

Chapter 27

The Direct Question

LET'S LOOK AT THE FOURTH CATEGORY, the direct question, and see how the Ledge can help us deal with that kind of response.

Sometimes, Critical Point #1 will take the form of a question like, "Okay, how much is it?" What happens next? Most of the time, the salesperson tries to dance around the question by saying things like, "Well, I'm going to get to that," or "That's one of the things I'm going to have to put together for you."

Salespeople usually say these things because they don't have enough information about the prospect yet to make any kind of intelligent recommendation; and without that information, they can't make any intelligent pricing decision. In other cases, salespeople know they're potentially vulnerable on the price front, and they don't want to handicap themselves by getting into specifics before they've discussed everything they offer in their product/service package. Most salespeople just want to avoid losing their momentum by spending ten minutes walking the prospect through a complicated pricing structure. For any of these reasons, salespeople try to dance around direct questions about price, and the pattern is very similar for direct questions that deal with other subjects.

The problem is that the person we called doesn't stop thinking about the question he or she just asked. While we're moving on to the next subject or the next question we want to ask, the person is thinking, "Gee, you called me, and I asked you a simple question and I can't get a simple answer. Why not?" The prospect has every reason to be unhappy with that, and as a result the call doesn't go well.

So when somebody asks you "How much is it?" you must be prepared with an answer. After all, you know you're going to get the question. You know the ball is coming your way. So you don't need to be surprised; you can prepare an answer and respond appropriately. I don't mean the *final* pricing answer, the one that will show up on the proposal. I mean a brief, truthful answer, a range, a ballpark estimate. And immediately after you respond to the person's question, you're going to pose a question of your own, just as you did with the request for information. Here's what it might sound like:

> *Well, Mr. Prospect, for a company in your industry, our prices are typically between A and B. Just out of curiosity, though, what are you doing right now to keep in touch with people who work out on the road?*

Create a Ledge by asking a question!

Remember—once you give an answer, you have the right to ask your own question! Do not pause for even an instant before asking that question. Regain control of the conversation by asking a question of your own about what the person does in some area that you feel you can eventually improve.

When you hear a "Direct Question " response, turn it around with the Ledge by briefly answering the question—perhaps by offering a price range—and immediately posing a question of your own.

Example: (How much does it cost?) The prices range between X per minute and Y per minute. I'm just curious, though, what overnight carrier are you using right now?

Action Item

Write down your own version of the turnaround you would use to handle a direct question. Respond briefly to the question and pose a question of your own. *Practice this turnaround out loud at least ten times.*

Keep reading to find out how to . . .

Chapter 28

Put It All Together

LET'S PUT TOGETHER WHAT WE'VE LEARNED about responses and turnarounds—and take a look at the Ledge in action. Suppose I call you on the phone and say this:

> *Jane Brown? Hi, Steve Schiffman. I'm with D.E.I. Management Group. We're a sales training company in—*

Suppose you cut me off instantly by saying this: "Sales training, eh? You know, I've just been put in charge of that. I'm really pressed for time today, though, Steve, so do you think you could just give me the thirty-second version of why you think we should be working with you?"

Obviously, that's Critical Point #1; you've just interrupted me. What's more, you've asked me a direct question. I have to get past that point if I'm going to have a conversation with you. Fortunately, I've already prepared a brief, factual answer for this question because it comes up all the time. I know ahead of time that I'm going to hear some variation of "Can you tell me why you think we should work with you?" So I say to you:

> *Sure, Jane. Basically, we've worked with a lot of companies in your industry, including This Company, That Company, and the Other Company, and we've been able to help their salespeople increase their total appointments by between 20 to 40 percent. I was just wondering, have you ever used sales training before?*

I've answered briefly and accurately, then posed a question of my own.

Now let's say you throw another fastball my way. You say: "Actually, Steve, we haven't used sales training before. The truth is, the president of the company has recently asked me to take a look at what we could consider doing in this area with an outside vendor. He wants me to put together a proposal that will cover the next ninety days. The problem is, though, that the companies in our industry that you just mentioned are much bigger than we are, and something tells me that they paid you a lot more than we could ever pay you. If you're working those kinds of companies, I think you're probably too expensive for us. We're just a small start-up."

What kind of response have I just heard? Of course, it's the "Not Interested" response.

So, what am I going to do next? I'm going to turn the objection around *and ask yet another question based on what the person or organization does.* In other words, I'm going to use the turnaround as a *bridge* to the next question I want to ask the person. This is the Ledge in action.

You know, a lot of people tell me that before they see how we can fit with a new budget. I'm just curious, what kinds of customers are you targeting?

If my aim were to secure a face-to-face appointment, I'd follow a slightly different pattern here. The contact would say something like, "I think you're probably too expensive for us; we're just a small start-up." I would then turn the objection around and say: "You know, a lot of our best customers said exactly the same thing before they saw how affordable we were. Just out of curiosity, how long have you been in business?" The prospect could then make any response, and I would position it as a reason for a meeting. For instance, I could say, "Oh, well if you've been in business for under a year, then we really should get together for a meeting, because we do a lot of work with companies in that category. I'd love to stop by and show you some of the programs we've put together; how's this Tuesday at three?" The same approach, of course, could be adapted to "phone meetings" and conference calls you schedule with prospects. (For more information on setting appointments, see my book *Cold Calling Techniques That Really Work!*)

The moment you ask the contact about what they're doing now, they are going to have to make some kind of response. Do you realize how much power that gives you? Suddenly, you're in control of the conversation—not because you're bullying the contact (you're not), but because you've made them respond!

The prospect may give you a negative response, but that's all right, because you know your four categories, and you're ready for any negative response that comes your way. In fact, if you stop and think about it, you'll probably realize that you've already got much more experience with negative responses than the people you call have in saying negative responses! Soon, the turnarounds will become second nature for you. It will be second nature for you to classify the response, turn it around appropriately, ask a question, and move smoothly from the opening of the conversation into the information-gathering step. All it takes is practice.

And that's the key word here: practice. Before you go on in the book, please practice the turnarounds you've learned. Get comfortable with them. Practice using them to get back to the extended conversation that allows you to find out what they do, how they do it, why they do it, when they do it, where they do it, who they do it with, and how you can help them do it better.

Action Item

Classify the ten common negative responses according to the turnaround categories.

Go back to the ten common negative responses you wrote down after reading Chapter 25. Classify each response according to the turnaround categories you've now learned. *Practice turning around each common response at least ten times out loud, using the strategies you've learned so far.*

Please do not proceed until you have completed the Action Item above. It's extremely important.

You'll notice that, up to this point, you've spent more time practicing the turnarounds than you have spent practicing your initial call approach. That's because I want you to learn about some alterations on the standard call before you start committing your approach to memory. Once you have completed the Action Item above, you'll be ready to learn about . . .

Chapter 29

Some Variations on the Standard Call

LET'S LOOK AT SOME ALTERNATE APPROACHES for scripting the opening of your call. We'll start by looking at how the third-party approach works. This is a highly effective variation on the basic script.

Suppose I'm already working with a large bank called the ABC Bank. And suppose I wish to call and get some business going with another bank, the XYZ Bank, a bank I have not done any work with yet. To make that call, I would follow the same three steps—attention, identification, and reason—but the words will change slightly so I can build in a reference to a third party, namely the ABC Bank. Here's what it might sound like:

Attention Statement: Good morning—Bob Ryan?

Identification Statement: This is Steve Schiffman. I'm with D.E.I. Management Group. We're a sales training company in New York, and we work with Company A, Company B, and Company C.

Reason for the Call: In fact, the reason I'm calling you today specifically is that we've just completed a very successful program with the ABC Bank. It was very instrumental in helping them achieve their sales goals this quarter. I'd like to talk to you about what we've done with ABC.

And assuming I had not yet been interrupted, I would proceed with my . . .

First Question: I'm just curious, have you ever worked with a sales training company before?

Please notice what I'm not doing. I'm not making the person feel like he's the four thousandth person I'm reciting my pitch to. (To the contrary, I'm focusing my call around the questions I hope this person can answer about what XYZ Bank has done in the past about sales training.) I'm also not saying, "We've done great work with ABC and I guarantee that I can do the exact same great work with you." (That would be premature.)

What I am doing is initiating a relationship, as one professional to another. In essence, I'm saying, "I am a professional with knowledge of your industry, and I've got some exciting information that I'd like to share with you. In fact, I think you might want to find out more about what we've done with ABC, and I might want to find out more about what you're doing."

The fact that I've done work with a similar bank says to the XYZ people, "Hey, I know something about your business. I have an experience that makes me credible as a possible supplier. I have some information I think is more likely to fit into what XYZ Bank does, and so I want to find out a little bit more about XYZ, and let them find out a little bit more about my organization as well."

Of course, in using the third-party approach, I have to be willing to give an overview of the work I've done with ABC Bank.

Ideally, that overview is going to be the initial focus of my call. All the same, I know that once I briefly outline what I've done with ABC, I'm going to come back to those questions. I'm going to try to find out what XYZ Bank is doing, has done in the past, and plans to do in the future. And when I hear an answer, I'm going to ask "How" and "Why" at every appropriate opportunity.

The third-party approach is an extremely effective variation on the standard calling model. In fact, it's so effective that most of the people we train eventually decide to adopt it. Once you're familiar with the basic call, you, too, may want to do a little research, find an appropriate third party within your company's customer base, build a new calling approach, and practice it until it's second nature to you.

Another important variation on the basic approach is the one we can use when we're working in an inbound telesales environment. In this case, the person is calling us; we're not initiating the call. Well, we still want to get the person to use what we have to offer. So our aim in this conversation is very similar, because we're still trying to move from the opening step into the information-gathering step. But we have to strategize the call somewhat differently.

The key here is to take your first opportunity to find out exactly why the person contacted you in the first place. In other words, something has changed in the prospect's world in order for him or her to reach out to us. The prospect didn't call because there was nothing better to do on a Monday morning. Our challenge is to find out what changed the status quo and led the person to initiate the call. So as soon as we can do so, we're going to ask a question that focuses on this.

Depending on your calling environment, the opening of the inbound call may take a variety of forms. Here are two very effective forms your approach can take in the inbound selling environment.

Hi, this is Bill Jones with Acme. How can I help you? (Prospect responds.) Okay—I was just curious, what made you decide to call us today?

Hi, this is Bill Jones with Acme. Can I get your account number? (Prospect responds.) Okay, and what is the reason for your call today? (Prospect responds.) All right. Well, you've reached the right place. (If appropriate:) Can I ask, though, what it was that made you decide to get in touch with us about that?

The idea is to find out *what's different now*—what the emotional reason for the call is. After all, something happened, otherwise the call would never have been placed. What was that event, and what decision did the prospect make as a result? Has this person just changed jobs? Been drafted into the military? Graduated from college? Purchased a car?

Action Item

Develop a final draft of your calling approach.

Use the basic approach, the third-party approach, or the inbound approach. Write down the actual words that you feel comfortable using as the opening of your call, and practice them out loud *at least twenty times before you proceed to Chapter 30.* You may want to record your practice sessions on a home tape recorder and critique your work before moving on with the rest of the program.

In the inbound call, your initial goal is to find out about the motivating event that inspired the call and to attempt to move from that question to another series of questions about what the person does. Remember, our goal is still to spend the vast majority of our time in the information-gathering phase. So if there are negative initial responses, we're going to turn them around and simply pose a question of our own.

Please do not proceed until you have completed the Action Item. It's extremely important. Once you've completed the exercise, you'll be ready to learn about . . .

Chapter 30

The Art of Leaving Messages

MOST SALESPEOPLE DON'T USE PERSONAL MESSAGES and voice-mail systems effectively. If you follow the advice you're about to read, you will get 65 to 90 percent return calls on the messages you leave.

Let's say that I've confirmed that I should call Mr. Smith of the XYZ Bank to talk about my product or service. When I call his company, though, he's not there. This means I'm liable to speak to either his secretary or his voice mail. If I speak to Mr. Smith's secretary, I'm in good shape. Why? Because the secretary typically has a script for handling messages, and I can anticipate what I'm going to hear. In fact, this script is already so familiar to me that I know the color of the paper the script is printed on. It's usually a pink piece of paper that has four blank spaces:

Name: ______________________________

Company: ___________________________

Phone number: ______________________________

Reason for the call: __________________________

Because I know the script ahead of time, I can have my answers ready. I'll say something like this:

(Name:) Please tell Mr. Smith that Steve Schiffman called.

(Company:) I'm with D.E.I. Management Group.

(Reason for the call:) I'm calling about the ABC Bank.

(Phone number:) My phone number is 212/555-1212.

Did you notice that I reversed the third and fourth items? They're in a sequence that is opposite from the one the secretary or receptionist is going to expect, based on that little pink piece of message paper. I'll explain that in a moment.

The main thing to notice is that, by giving the ABC Bank as the reason for my call, I am substantially increasing the odds that I'll get a call back. What I've done here is to adapt the third-party approach to my phone message; ABC Bank is a bank in Mr. Smith's industry that I've recently done business with. (This could also be a bank Mr. Smith has done business with, one that is close to him geographically, one with a national reputation, or simply one he's familiar with.)

I don't even leave a message unless I know what my third-party endorsement is going to be! On the other hand, if I have to leave a message, I'm ready to do that. "What's the call in reference to?" It's in reference to the ABC Bank. That's what I want to talk about with Mr. Smith.

Now, the reason I gave the last two pieces of information out of the order that the typical secretary would expect is that, given a choice, I would rather not try to sell to the secretary. In fact, I would rather not engage the secretary in any kind of extended conversation. So reversing the order of the information is my strategy or what the behavioral scientists call a "pattern interrupt." It's going to throw the secretary off ever so slightly and give me the opportunity to leave the message—and conclude the call—on my own terms.

Follow it out. If I said, as my last comment, that the reason for my call was the ABC Bank, the secretary would be more likely to react to that and say, "Well, wait a minute—what do you mean by that? What about the ABC Bank?" At that point, I would have to go into a whole discussion about the ABC Bank with the secretary that I really don't want to have. So by interrupting her pattern and giving the information just slightly out of order, I stand a better chance of maintaining control with the call.

If I happen to get voice mail, I can use the very same approach. I can say who I am, what company I'm calling from, the reason for my call ("I'm calling in regard to the ABC Bank"), and my return number. *That's it. Nothing more.*

Follow this strategy and I promise that you will be amazed at the number of return calls you get. The people we train typically get a minimum 65 percent call-back rate.

There's another strategy that can get you a 90 percent-plus return-call rate, but it only works with someone you've had trouble connecting with (or reconnecting with) for quite some time. It's a lead-swapping strategy you must execute in partnership with someone else in your office.

Here's how it works. Look back over your records and get the numbers of all the people who haven't returned your calls for at least a month. Then team up with another sales rep who has done the same thing. Swap phone numbers.

Let's say the person you swapped with is named Bart. You would then call all of Bart's people who didn't return calls and leave a simple message:

> *(Name:) Hi, this is Jim Franklin.*
>
> *(Company:) I'm calling from Acme Widget . . .*
>
> *(Reason for the call:) . . . regarding Bart Smith.*
>
> *(Phone number:) Please call me at 212/555-1212 as soon as possible.*

Notice that you make Bart Smith the reason for your call. (Bart is, at the same time, making you the reason for his calls to the people who wouldn't call back.) When people start calling you back—and they will—here's what you'll say:

> *Mr. Jones—thanks for calling me back. I was calling regarding Bart Smith. My records show that he called you a while back to talk about the work we'd done with ABC Bank. Anyway . . .*

Now, the reason people will return your call in the first place is that they will be vaguely concerned about poor Bart. Why on earth has someone left a message about *him*? Is something wrong? During these calls, the most remarkable thing will happen. *People will start to defend Bart.*

"It's really nothing Bart did," they'll say. "The problem was on our end. We had a hiring freeze here last quarter, and we really couldn't even look at anything like that until this month." And at that point a whole new conversation will open up.

This message strategy has resulted in over 90 percent return call rates! Try it yourself and see what happens.

Action Item

Review your list of contacts and identify at least ten people you have had difficulty connecting with. Use one of the two strategies in this chapter to leave an effective message.

As you've no doubt noticed, building your call around a satisfied customer is an important part of this program. It's not the *only* way to connect with potential customers over the phone, however. Read on to find out about . . .

Chapter 31

Another Effective Variation

THE THIRD-PARTY ENDORSEMENT is a very effective way to make a call or leave a message, but what do you do if you have no such party endorsement? Suppose you have no customers within a given industry segment?

For one thing, you can highlight work you've done with people in a given geographical area. You can also focus on large companies your contact is likely to have heard of, regardless of the industry such companies occupy. You can even build your approach around any satisfied customer in your base or around a company your organization has done work for at no charge! These aren't necessarily my first choices in developing a telesales approach, but the truth is that many people we've worked with have used ideas like these to develop extremely effective calling campaigns.

Here's another interesting variation to consider—take the opposite approach. Instead of saying that you may be in a position to help Mr. Smith's business because of all your past experience in a certain area, admit that you don't know a lot about Mr. Smith's business, and work from there. It sounds like an unlikely approach for making contact, and yet we've found that it can be incredibly effective. This is what it might sound like:

(Attention statement:) Hi, Mr. Smith.

(Identification statement:) This is Steve Schiffman from D.E.I. Management Group. We're a sales training firm here in New York City.

(Reason for the call:) The reason I'm calling you today specifically is that we are thinking of marketing to companies in the widget industry. We think it makes sense because a lot of our trainers have employment experience in the hoober industry, which is similar, but frankly, we don't know a lot about widgets. So I was wondering if I could talk to you about what we offer, find out what you do, and then see whether there's a match.

We've completely changed the nature of the call. It sounds like an upper-level, consultative discussion. This approach can work very well, in part because we come off sounding more direct and more honest. If we say that we're thinking of marketing to a certain group, that's certainly true. That's what we're always trying to do! And as far as looking for a match, that's a very honest description of what sales is all about, too. Sometimes we find a match; sometimes we don't.

Here's the irony: This "no-experience-in-your-industry" call will probably be perceived as slightly more upscale than the average telesales call. That's because this approach assumes a somewhat more professional-sounding tone than the standard call. You'll still get negative responses, and you'll still have to turn them around and ask questions, but you may well find that this twist is the most appropriate for your selling environment.

Action Item

Develop and practice an alternate draft based on the principles in this chapter. Practice it and determine whether it makes sense for your selling environment.

One of the immutable rules of the game we're playing is that *no* calling approach can deliver a great conversation with each and every decision-maker you target. Sometimes, you'll have to follow up on calls that seem promising, but don't yield a prospect.

Read on to find out how to master . . .

Chapter 32

The Art of Calling Back

SUPPOSE YOU'VE CALLED SOMEBODY at one point in the year—say, August 1—and the person says, "Why don't you call me again in September?"

Fundamentally, of course, this is a "not interested" response. So you'll attempt to turn that around, and sometimes you'll do so and you'll actually initiate a conversation. But sometimes you won't be able to turn the response around. What do you do?

Well, the first thing to do is to ask the prospect "Why?" In other words, you'll try a few times to get a conversation going. (We recommend attempting to turn an initial negative response around three times.) Assume, though, that you hit a brick wall, and the person says, "No, I really want you to call me back in September." Instead of just saying, "Okay, September it is," try saying this:

Sure. I can make a note and give you a call back in September. How's September 1?

You set a date. You gather whatever information you can. The call concludes. What happens next?

First and foremost, you write yourself a message to call back on September 1 and jot down the most important points of your conversation. The first of September rolls around; you check your date book or computer; you see the note to call your contact. You pick up the phone and you say something like this:

Hi, Mr. Smith. This is Steve Schiffman. When we last spoke, on August 1, you asked me to give you a call today.

That's it. Stop talking. Throw the ball out and see what happens. Some kind of response will come your way. The person might say, "Gee, I have no recollection of that conversation." You could then continue with:

Well, I was telling you all about the great work we've been doing with ABC. We were very successful in helping them achieve their goals. I'm just curious, have you ever worked with a sales training company before?

Can you see how it works? Use the "you asked me to call" approach as your opening. Whatever negative response you hear, turn it around and use it as a platform for a "do-based" question.

Action Item

Identify ten people in your contact base who asked you to call back at least one month in the future. Use the principles in this chapter to reestablish contact with as many of those ten people as you can.

Selling over the phone is a matter of igniting—or reigniting—interest in an in-depth conversation. In the next chapter, you'll learn about a single sentence that helps you to do just that with all kinds of people you may have called in the past. The words to remember are . . .

Chapter 33

"I Was Just Thinking of You"

SO FAR, WE'VE TALKED A LOT ABOUT COLD CALLS. But not every call we make is going to be to someone we've never spoken to before. Suppose we want to call an existing customer we haven't spoken to in a long time. Or we want to call a lead we feel pretty good about, somebody we've become friendly with from a series of phone calls but who has never actually bought anything from us. How do you get these people on the phone if you have no actual reason to call?

The truth is, you always have a reason to call. In these situations, you can call your customer or your warm lead and simply say:

> *Hi Bill, it's Steve Schiffman. I was thinking of you and I thought I'd give you a call.*

Simple, isn't it? And yet this has got to be one of the most powerful conversational openings when it comes to reawakening dormant contacts. This opening is 100 percent accurate, not misleading in the slightest, extremely flattering, and remarkably flexible. You can take this opening and make it very elaborate. ("I was just thinking about that talk we had last month and wondering whether you'd solved that payroll problem you were grappling with.") Or you can keep it simple. ("You know what? I was just thinking about you and decided to check in.") In either case, you'll throw out the ball and see what comes back.

Try it—you'll be amazed at how well it works. Nine times out of ten, the simple act of calling and saying "I was just thinking of you" to someone you already know will initiate a good conversation with the person. Very often, the person will say, "You know, it's interesting that you'd call right now, because I happen to be looking at such-and-such a problem, and I was going to call you to talk about it, but I just never made the time." Your call triggers a positive exchange!

Note, too, that you can use "I was just thinking of you" as the basis of a voice-mail message. You'll be amazed at the calls you get back!

Sometimes, when I train salespeople in the "I was just thinking of you" technique, they tell me, "Steve, that's great for *some* situations, but what about people who've had a problem with our company, people who used to be customers?" Keep reading to find out . . .

Action Item

Use this approach with three people in your contact base.

Look through your contact base. How many people within it represent dormant opportunities you could reawaken using the principle outlined in this chapter? Call at least three of these people and tell them, "I was just thinking of you."

Chapter 34

How to Call Former Customers

WHAT DO YOU DO WHEN YOU want to reinitiate your relationship with somebody who used to buy from you but stopped for some reason?

The point of this call is to find out what stopped them from buying from you. Get to that issue first. Here's what it might sound like:

Hi, Ms. Brown, this is Steve Schiffman from D.E.I. Management Group. I'll tell you the reason I wanted to get in touch with you today. We haven't heard from you in a long time, and I was wondering if there was something wrong.

What happens when I say that? It triggers a response. Suppose there was nothing wrong other than the fact that the person simply had no reason to call. I may hear, "Gee, there's really no problem at all, Steve. I've just been busy." Now I know there's no big, burning issue that prevents us from doing business together. There's no reason. I'm just doing something else. I can pick up instantly with something like this:

Oh, well, Ms. Brown, I'm glad I called anyway, because we've just completed a very successful prospect management program with ABC Bank, and I wanted to tell you about it. But I'm just curious—what are you doing to reach out to new customers right now?

Where do I end up? With a "do-based" question! You're getting the idea by now, right? *Virtually every response we get over the phone is an opportunity to redirect the conversation toward a "do-based" question.* In a heartbeat, we're gathering information and building a good conversation.

Now suppose Ms. Brown tells me, "Well, actually, Steve, the reason that I haven't called is that we're very upset. We had this problem with you last time." What can I do?

First of all, I'm going to recognize that if that issue really will prevent us from doing business, and I honestly can't solve that issue, the conversation is pretty much over. I'm going to apologize, disengage politely, and avoid spending an unnecessary amount of time on that phone call. I'll be able to move on to my next call, which is really fine. On the other hand, suppose I find out that the issue that's bothering Ms. Brown is something that used to be a problem, but that I can actually help resolve now. I'll be able to say to her:

Ms. Brown, a lot of people who had that problem a year or so ago are now back with us again because they found that we've changed. I'd love to be able to help solve this problem. In a perfect world, what would you like to see us do in this area?

I may or may not be able to deliver on everything Ms. Brown wants, but with a question like that, she'll have no doubt whatsoever that I'm on her side and I want to rebuild the relationship!

Action Item

Identify at least one former customer you can contact using the principles outlined in this chapter.

Call that person, and open the conversation by saying something along the following lines: "We haven't heard from you in a while, and I was wondering whether there was something wrong."

I've used the very strategy you just learned to contact presidents and CEOs—and to renew relationships that ended up being worth hundreds of thousands of dollars. We train people to call as high in the organizational hierarchy as is practical for them. In other words, if the president of your target company *can* benefit from what you have to offer, and thereby make the decision for you, you should probably start out by calling the president's office. Learn how to do that effectively by discovering . . .

Chapter 35

How to Get and Use Connections with People at the Top

AT THE VERY END OF THE LAST CHAPTER, I discussed the possibility of calling the most senior-level person who could benefit from your product or service.

Let's assume that you call that person. For the purposes of example, we'll call him Mr. El Grande. He's the president of your target organization. Whenever you call people at the very top of the organization, you'll find that they frequently suggest that you call some lower-echelon person. In this case, we'll assume that that's exactly what happens. You connect with Mr. El Grande, and he very quickly suggests you to call that subordinate of his, Mr. Lowe.

Suppose you want another shot at a good conversation with Mr. El Grande during this call—without jeopardizing your chance to use Mr. El Grande when you talk to Mr. Lowe later on. Before you conclude your call, say something like the following.

Well, Mr. El Grande, thank you for giving me Mr. Lowe's name; I'll call him if you think it would help. But I've been talking to your counterparts, other presidents at other large widget companies, and I'd like to tell you what I've been telling them.

Not always, but a good percentage of the time, you'll actually have a good conversation with Mr. El Grande. Suppose, though, that that doesn't happen, and Mr. El Grande simply says, "You know what? You really are going to have to speak to Mr. Lowe because he handles everything in this area for me." What do you do then? Here's how to get the very most from the referral. You call Mr. Lowe and say:

Hi, Mr. Lowe. This is Steve Schiffman from D.E.I. Management Group in New York City. Mr. El Grande said you were the right person for me to talk to.

You've thrown out the ball. Mr. Lowe has to respond somehow. Typically, he'll respond by saying, "Okay, what's it about?" (It's pretty rare that a top-level referral like this will encourage the person to brush you off immediately. You're likely to get a question before you reach Critical Point #1.) Once Mr. Lowe says, "Okay, what's it about?" You can then say, "Well, we've just completed a very successful program with the ABC Company . . ." At some point, you're going to get a negative response. Mr. Lowe is going to say something like this: "Steve, I've looked at companies like yours, and I'm afraid we really can't afford that."

What's the turnaround? You know it already, don't you?

You know, ABC said the same thing before they saw how we could work within their budget. I'm just curious, what other companies have you been looking at?

You're gathering information.

Let me show you a more enhanced version of the same referral strategy. You speak to Mr. El Grande, and he says, "It all sounds fascinating, and I'm glad you're talking to other presidents in the widget industry, but you really are going to have to call Mr. Lowe." So you ask for Mr. Lowe's direct number and find some way to initiate that call yourself. You politely disengage from any attempt Mr. El Grande may make to connect you directly with Mr. Lowe, for reasons that will become obvious in a moment.

Ten seconds or so after you speak to Mr. El Grande, you call Mr. Lowe directly and set the stage for a discussion that focuses on what his organization actually does. You'll do that by saying:

Hi, Mr. Lowe, this is Steve Schiffman calling from D.E.I. Management Group. Did Mr. El Grande tell you I'd be calling? He didn't? Well, let me tell you what we were talking about. I was telling Mr. El Grande all about the great work we've been doing with ABC Company. We helped their reps to schedule 35 percent more programs in just two weeks. Anyway, Mr. El Grande said you were the person I should connect with about this. I'm curious, have you ever worked with a sales training company before?

Action Item

Call the president of at least one company you hope to sell to and, using the strategies outlined in this chapter, attempt to initiate contact or generate a referral. Repeat the process at least three times.

If you follow the advice in this chapter, you'll use the referral from a high-level contact to inject a massive dose of enthusiasm and energy and urgency into the call. Energy and enthusiasm are incredibly important factors in your sales success—whether you're making this kind of call or any other connection over the phone. To find out why it's so important to project enthusiasm on the phone, read Chapter 36, and discover . . .

Chapter 36

How to Send the Right Emotional Message over the Phone

NINETY-NINE PERCENT OF ALL TELEMARKETERS use the first few seconds of a call to send an emotional message that doesn't match up with the actual words they're saying.

Please understand: I'm not talking about the approach (script) they've developed. The literal content of the words they're reciting during that precious three- or four-second time span—"Hi, I'm calling from Acme Company, and I wanted to tell you about a very exciting program we just put together for one of our clients."—may be fine. However, the emotional message they're conveying is sometimes closer to "Hi there—I really wish I hadn't made this phone call."

Right words, wrong tonality. Guess how the person who receives the call interprets that opening? You guessed right. Tonality wins almost every time. The contact is perfectly justified in responding, "You know what? I, too, wish you hadn't made this phone call."

Throughout this book, I've emphasized the importance of asking questions in order to gather information from the prospect and initiate a good first call, or Initial Contact. It's certainly true that asking questions is vitally important. But you have to be very careful about how you phrase the questions and what tone of voice you use to deliver them!

At this point in my career, I've listened to literally hundreds of thousands of salespeople ask questions. All too often, what I hear sounds like a survey question, a question that's delivered with all the enthusiasm of a resident of the city morgue. "Hi, I'm sorry to bother you, and I won't take up too much of your time, but we now have an ABC component to our products. Are you interested?" The person says, "No, actually, I'm not in the least interested in that," and it's on to the next call. "Hi, I hope I haven't called at a bad time, but my company offers the XYZ option. Do you care?" "Actually, since you mentioned it, this is a lousy time to call, and no, I don't care at all about that."

With that kind of question structure and that kind of tonality, we might as well be asking, "Hi, I'm currently under sedation and I hate my job. I'm calling you in order to waste your time and keep you from getting to the things on your to-do list. I just had a question for you—do you happen to know what the population of North Dakota was in 1948? You don't?"

Be sure your questions are intelligently structured. Be sure people get an emotional message that matches and supports the words of your approach. This is very important, because the emotional message you send for the first few seconds of the call will have a powerful effect on the messages you get back. People respond in kind, remember?

Do not send an emotional message that says "I wish I were doing something else." Instead, it has to be something like this.

"Are you sitting down? No? Then find a chair, bolt it to the floor, take a seat, and prepare to be utterly and completely blown away, because what I'm about to tell you has the potential to completely transform your business and your life. This is the most important and exciting call you're going to get all day. Let's get ready to RRRRRRRRRUMBLE!"

Action Item

Find *your* emotional message.

Practice your calling approach again. Tape-record the words you would say during the first few seconds of the call and ask someone else to listen to the result. Then ask him or her, "What emotional message is coming across?" Record the answer in your notebook.

You now have all the tools you need to initiate the telesales call effectively. After a brief brush-up of what you've learned, you'll be ready to find out about . . .

Chapter 37

The Recipe for a Great Conversation

IT'S TIME FOR A QUICK REVIEW of the key concepts we've covered. If we were to map out what we've done in the call so far, it would look something like this:

- Hello/Approach. If we're calling in an outbound selling environment, what we've done is to *initiate* the call—say "Hello," if you will—by using an attention statement, a reason for the call, and (in the unlikely event we are not interrupted) a question. (In an inbound selling environment, we're going to try to find out what has *changed* in the caller's world to inspire his or her decision to call us.)
- Response. This is Critical Point #1. There's an initial negative response. If we don't get past this instinctive, knee-jerk response, which may sound very convincing but is really superficial, we have nothing.

- Turnaround. Take the initial negative response and turn it around. Regardless of the many variations of this we may hear, there are really only four categories for the initial negative response. In Chapters 24 through 28, we learned how to turn around each of the response categories. *Immediately* after turning around the response, we will ask a . . .
- Question. If the person answers our question and engages in a real conversation with us, then we classify the exchange as an Initial Contact—a good first conversation. Initial Contacts lead to Prospects, and Prospects lead to Sales.

Clearly, it is in our best interests to turn as many of our calls into Initial Contacts as possible. The question is, How exactly do we do that?

Well, you'll remember that we've already looked at the *kinds* of questions we want to ask during these conversations—"do-based" questions. Now it's time to look at how the conversation itself should be structured.

At my company, we've monitored hundreds of thousands of sales conversations over the years, and we've found that sometimes salespeople have *great* conversations with the people they want to sell to and sometimes they don't. Armed with this seemingly obvious piece of information—some calls are great, others aren't—we asked ourselves a simple question: What do the great calls have in common? We found that *great sales conversations follow a predictable outline.*

Once the conversation has moved from the opening step into the information-gathering step, the best conversations with prospects are going to follow a very clear pattern. Here it is:

- Parable
- Information

- Present options
- Ask directly for a Next Step

We call this the P-I-P-A sequence. Let's look at it in depth.

Present a brief commercial. We have to position ourselves in such a way that we offer a little bit of information about our organization—or respond to the other person's concern or question with a relevant story or parable. Then we can pose a question of our own.

Notice that we are not talking about asking for permission by saying, "Do you mind if I ask you a few questions?" Instead, we're going to assume that we have won permission by offering information in a relevant area . . . and then pose a question of our own. Here's how that works at the very beginning of the relationship—at the start of the first conversation.

Say I call the president of a software company and initially the call seems to be going pretty well. I want to get permission to ask a question about how our contact got started at his or her company. In that situation, I might start by saying, "Would it help if I told you a little bit about my organization and myself?" Usually, the person responds by saying, "Sure, go ahead." Watch what happens next:

> *Okay. D.E.I. Management Group is a sales training company. We've been around since 1979, we've trained nearly half a million individuals around the world, and we've worked with just about every industry, from telecommunications to health care to entertainment to advertising to industrial companies and information companies. And I personally conduct over 200 programs per year to thousands of salespeople in the United States and in other countries. Can I ask, though—how does someone become the president of a software company?*

What have I done? I've just shared a little bit about what the company does and a little bit about what I do. (Note that I haven't thrown up on the prospect.) I've followed that with a question, because by saying what I do, I have automatically won permission to ask something about the other person. And this particular question—"How does someone go about becoming a (whatever)?"—is one that people invariably love to answer.

Information. Once the conversation is underway, we ask more questions and begin to gain the information we're after. We must listen carefully, which is more difficult than it sounds. The other person's responses must affect the content of our subsequent questions. Even though we're directing the conversation, we can't simply recite a prewritten list of queries as though we were working for the Gallup Poll. Notice that the question topics and suggestions you read about earlier are for the purpose of helping you to develop your *initial* question. Those lists should not be used as a checklist, an unchanging sequence of questions that overwhelm the prospect! Our aim is to make sure the questions follow logically, based on what the other person says.

Present options. When we have gathered enough information, we can present some Next Step option or range of Next Step options that will keep us working with the prospect. Such a Next Step option could take many forms. It could be to close the sale, or it could simply be to speak again at some mutually agreed upon date and time. If we're presenting a number of options, we'll want to work with the prospect to identify the best one and then . . .

Ask directly for commitment. After we've presented that option—whatever it is—we will ask directly and specifically for a commitment from the prospect. We won't say, "You know, I really ought to put together a summary of what we could do for you, and then I think we ought to talk about that sometime." Instead, we'll say, "I'd like to fax you a one-page outline that would give you an idea of what our formal proposal would look like, and then I'd like to set up a time for us to talk about that outline. How's tomorrow at three?" By focusing on a specific date and time for a future discussion with the prospect, you change the focus from whether the two of you will talk again to when you will talk again.

Action Item

Practice asking for the Next Step.

Review the P-I-P-A sequence closely. Next Step. Develop a script or approach in which you deliver a *very brief* description of your product or service, then ask something about the other person. Develop another script or approach in which you ask specifically for a Next Step option that's relevant to your selling environment. Then, on your own, rehearse these pieces out loud, remembering to keep your self-description concise and to ask directly and clearly for contact at a specific date and time.

Keep reading to find out about the critical areas you will explore during the interview, including . . .

Chapter 38

The Past, the Present, and the Future

YOU'VE JUST LEARNED THE BEST MODEL for gathering information from the prospect.

If we use that P-I-P-A model to uncover what has happened, is happening, and will happen in the prospect's world, then the person we're talking to will remain interested in the conversation. Notice that this is a proactive conversation model. That means that, at various points, we will keep presenting options until the other person either agrees to some clear Next Step with us or one or the other of us decides not to pursue the process any further. (For more on when to disengage from a prospect, see Chapter 43.)

Understand, however, that even though we are asking directly for a Next Step once we have gathered sufficient information, we are not using a "hard sell" approach on the prospect. Using P-I-P-A means we talk a little, and they talk a little, we talk a little, and they talk a little. Both parties listen to each other. Both parties get to react. Both parties agree on the Next Step.

We are not trying to convince anyone of anything. Quite the contrary! In order to make a recommendation that really works, in order to suggest something that does, in fact, fit into what the other person is doing and how he or she does it, we have to forget about trying to convince people about how great we are. Instead, we have to focus on the past, the present, and the future and then listen extremely closely to what the other person says. This is the very opposite of the traditional "hard sell" philosophy.

We also have to avoid two very common mistakes associated with the "hard sell." The first mistake is that of "throwing up" on the prospect. In other words, we're not going to ask a single question, get an answer, and then take over the conversation so we can recite our brochure to the person for five minutes straight. A lot of salespeople do this. They pose a question simply as a trick, as an excuse to get the other person to respond so they can do what we call a "product dump." It sounds like this: "I'm glad you mention service contracts, Mr. Jones. We've been a leader in that field for the last seventy years. You see, Acme Company was founded in 1931 by Martin Acme, and guiding his philosophy was . . . " Now the salesperson is no longer gathering information but rather reciting a monologue.

This brings us to the second mistake of the "hard sell," the rapport-destroying "Always Be Closing" trap. Upon completing a product dump, many salespeople will fall into this sales-killing trap. They'll ask for the order, ask for the order, and ask for the order—regardless of whether or not they actually know anything about what the other person does. "They offer you overnight delivery? Oh, well we offer that, too. Now, would you rather start on Monday or Tuesday?"

By using the P-I-P-A model to focus on the prospect's past, present, and future, we're going to steer clear of both of these problems. We're engaging in a reciprocal conversation—one in which we are trading answers with the prospect and giving each other permission to continue. We're not monopolizing the conversation. And by presenting options that are actually based on what we've heard about what the prospect is hoping to accomplish, we're going to be sure the Next Step we ask for is one that matches what the other person does. As a result, we won't need those manipulative closing techniques.

In fact, at D.E.I. we teach only one closing technique. We have just one way to ask for the order at the end of the sale. It sounds like this:

"It makes sense to me. What do you think?"

That closing technique is the exact opposite of the various "hard sell" closes. Suppose we ask all about the past, the present, and the future. Suppose we gather our information and, at a certain point in the sales cycle—it could be the first call, it could be the fifth call—we say, "Based on what you've told me, this is my recommendation. I think it makes sense for us to work together. What do you think?" By doing that, we've asked for a Next Step. Specifically, in this case, we've asked for a commitment to work with this prospect.

What happens next? Well, the prospect may say, "Yes, it does make sense," in which case we've just closed the sale. On the other hand, the prospect may also say, "You know what—it really doesn't make sense to me and here's why." The point is that the response we get tells us *exactly* what steps we've missed, if any. In most cases, the prospect's response to the "makes sense" close will tell us whether or not we should continue trying to develop a recommendation for this person.

Look at it again. You say to me, "It makes sense to me. What do you think?" What is it about what you're suggesting that will make sense to me? The answer is simple: *A plan*, or *proposal*, or *presentation* that matches what I'm actually doing. Only if you suggest something that matches what I'm trying to get accomplished will I conclude that we have a reason to work together.

Now, what is it about that reason to work together that makes sense to me? What is your proposal based on? Of course: You based it on the *information* you collected from me. Look again at the sales process:

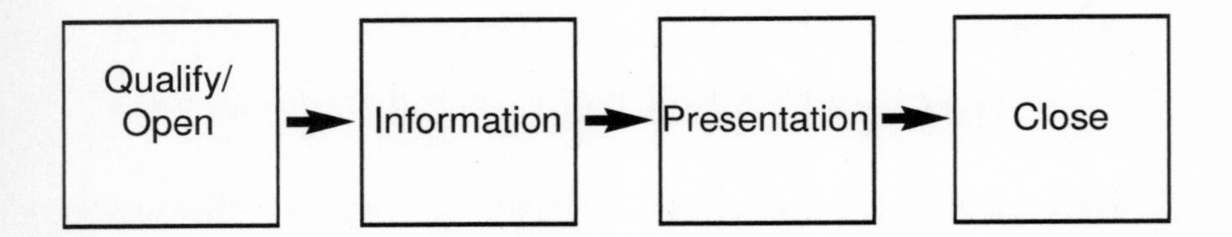

You were able to figure out what I do, how I do it, why I do it, where I do it, what my organization is doing, what I as an individual am doing, and who my professional allies are. You know this because you've asked about . . .

- What I have done in the *past*
- What I'm doing in the *present*
- What I'm planning to do in the *future.*

This is exactly what the interview must be focused on: what the prospect did in the past, what the prospect is doing right now, and what the prospect wants to see happen in the future. If we focus our interview step on these points, the plan will make sense to the prospect because it came from the prospect. We will include things that make sense to our contact–and leave out everything else. At that point, the "hard sell" will be obsolete.

Action Item

Write down at least fifteen questions you would like to ask your prospects. Focus each question on what the person (or organization) did in the past in that area, is currently doing, and hopes to make happen.

In addition to posing questions about the past, the present, and the future, you must also make it a point to . . .

Chapter 39

Ask "How" and "Why" Early and Often

WE'VE SEEN THE IMPORTANCE OF ASKING ABOUT THE PAST, the present, and the future. Here's another way to focus your questions effectively: Before you make *any* recommendation for *any* kind of Next Step, a*sk how and why questions.* This is a simple, vitally important principle that nine out of ten salespeople ignore completely. The concept is so essential to sales success that I'm devoting an entire chapter to it here.

Assume that you sell widgets and you've hooked up with the Vice President of Widgets, Jane Powers. Assume you've successfully turned around her initial negative response and gotten past Critical Point #1. You've started to ask Jane some questions; she's started to ask you some questions. A good conversation seems to be underway.

I say "seems" because you do not yet know enough about Jane's role in the organization to classify this conversation as an Initial Contact. So far, Jane *sounds* like the person who handles widget acquisition, and her job title would lead you to believe that she *should* handle widget acquisition. You might be tempted to *assume* that she either handles widget acquisition or is closely connected to someone who does. But you don't know for sure, so you should not yet try to set up a Next Step with her.

The way most salespeople would try to confirm Jane's status or role in the organization would be to ask, "Tell me, Jane, who's in charge of buying widgets at your company? Is that you?" The problem with that approach is that we haven't built up enough of a relationship with Jane yet for her to be able to trust us with the correct answer to that question. We just called her. It's very likely that she'll respond instinctively by saying, "Oh, yes, that's me"—regardless of her actual role in the decision-making process.

A much better way to uncover information about Jane's status or role is to pose some variation on this question sequence:

Jane, I'm curious—how did you choose ABC Widget?

Who else did you talk to? Why them?

What was it that made you finally decide to work with ABC?

This is a *how* and *why* question sequence. If Jane knows the answer, she will probably tell you, and you'll be well on your way to getting the information you need. If Jane *doesn't* know how the decision was made last time, *you are not talking to the right person!* You need to keep moving through the organization (either with Jane's help or without it) in order to track down the true decision-maker *or* someone who can get the decision made in your favor.

We have a saying at my office: "Ask how and why, and the who will emerge." If you always ask how and why questions before recommending a Next Step, you will spend less of your precious time presenting to the wrong people.

Action Item

Do a simple role-play. Practice asking "how" and "why" question sequences with your sales manager or one of your colleagues.

In the next chapter, you'll find out why it's important to . . .

Chapter 40

Verify Your Information

MANY OF THE SALESPEOPLE WE TRAIN like to build their Next Step around an outline or preliminary proposal. This is a document—typically only one or two pages long—that enables you to raise key issues *before* you make a formal recommendation. In other words, an outline is a document that says to the prospect, "I am not a proposal—go ahead and change me, scribble all over me, revise my priorities."

There are three big advantages to using an outline or preliminary proposal in a telesales setting. First, it gives you an automatic reason to schedule a second or subsequent call. Again, that's the "A" in the P-I-P-A sequence, asking directly for a Next Step. It could sound like this: "I'd like to fax you a one-page outline of what I'd build our formal proposal around and then schedule another call for tomorrow afternoon at three so we can talk it over. How does that sound?"

The second major advantage of using a preliminary proposal

is that it serves as a signal to the prospect that you will soon be asking for their business. You're not asking right now—after all, this is only a preliminary proposal—but you will be asking once your prospect has had the chance to give you his or her reaction. So when you do ask to work with this person, that request won't come as a surprise.

The most important advantage to the preliminary proposal is that it allows you to incorporate corrections and verbatim feedback from the prospect within your formal recommendation. Whether that recommendation takes the form of a fourteen-page written document or a verbal summary of key points, the plan should be structured around the actual corrections and changes the outline has helped you to uncover. This process of getting corrected is known as "verifying information." It's a necessary prerequisite to moving forward to the presentation step, whether or not you use a written outline as a selling tool.

All too often, salespeople worry about making a mistake the prospect will notice and correct. Actually they should be trying to find a way *to make such a mistake*. That sounds like a strange thing to say, but hear me out. We cannot be sure we are right until we are righted. When we get the prospect to correct us, we know that we're on the right track. So in a way, it's right to be wrong! Getting righted is what the verification step is all about. Verifying our information means getting corrected about:

- Our assumptions and eventual recommendation
- Our contact (Is this person actually the decision-maker? Is someone else involved?)
- The dollar amount we're proposing
- The timetable for delivery or implementation

The outline is a tool for setting out what we believe to be true in each of these four areas. Many of the telesales professionals we've worked with have embraced it as an extremely effective way to verify information *and* determine whether or not a contact is willing to continue playing ball. Of course, if your selling environment requires you to try to close the sale during a single call, faxing or mailing an outline would not be appropriate. But using intelligent questions to verify your information in all four of the above areas is appropriate. In fact, it's essential.

Do not make a presentation to do business with a prospect before you verify your information!

Action Item

Verify information with a current prospect.

If it's appropriate to your selling environment, write a simple outline or preliminary proposal you could send to a current prospect. If your selling environment requires a closing attempt on a single call, develop at least three questions you can use to check information with a current prospect. In either case, be sure you verify *key assumptions,* the role of the *decision-maker* or *contact* you're working with, the *dollar value* of the deal you're proposing, and the *timetable* for implementation.

You're ready to learn about the third step in the sales cycle. Turn to the next chapter to find out how smoothly the *proposal* or *presentation* step can move forward when you . . .

Chapter 41

Paint a Picture

BASED ON WHAT WE HEAR and verify during the interview step, we will start to present some options of what could happen next in the relationship. The Next Step we ask for could be another information-gathering call. It could also be a *proposal* or presentation about how we might actually work with the prospect. And eventually, of course, that's what we want to do. We want to move forward in the sales process and make a recommendation that makes sense based on all the information we've gathered.

Earlier in the book, you learned that our conversation must be interesting to the person we're talking to and that the way to make it interesting is to focus on what that person does. In addition, we have to help the other person visualize what our services can do and how they fit into his or her environment. This visualization process is one of the best ways to move from the information-gathering step into the *proposal* or presentation step.

One great way to help the other person paint a picture is to practice what we call *parable selling*. That is, we promote our product or service by telling a relevant story rather than by trying to convince anyone of anything. Our experience is that the single best way to make the transition out of information and into some kind of presentation is to tell a true story about how your products fit into other companies that face similar situations, similar issues, and similar dilemmas.

So let's say we're talking to Mr. Andrews about distance learning programs—training programs that don't require that participants be in the same room, or the same city, as the trainer. Suppose Mr. Andrews mentions that his company is expanding its sales force in four different cities at once, and he's not sure how to train them all without shattering his travel budget. As it happens, we have some products that could benefit a company in that situation. We'll paint a picture for Mr. Andrews by saying something like this:

> *Do you know what? Just last month I was working with another company, Global Industries, that was expanding its sales force in a number of different cities at the same time, just as you're doing. They faced issues A, B, and C, and we were able to overcome those potential obstacles by doing X, Y, and Z. As a result, they were able to beat their quota in six brand-new offices in the first quarter after they learned what we taught them through distance learning.*

Suddenly, it's much easier for Mr. Andrews to visualize how my company's distance learning products could benefit his organization. By focusing on a relevant, accurate success story, we've laid the groundwork to give Mr. Andrews either a formal written presentation or a brief preliminary proposal that will help us get verbatim feedback and lead to a final recommendation. In a one-call close environment, a parable can lead directly to the close: "Based on what you've told me so far, I think it makes sense to get that kind of program started for your organization. What do you think?"

Action Item

Prepare at least six accurate, verifiable success stories based on your organization's customers. Write them in your notebook.

Use your success stories to get all the prospect's issues right out on the table so you can address them directly. ("ABC Company had a very similar concern, and here's how we handled it . . .") Remember, it should not come as a surprise to the prospect when you ask for their business! Keep reading to find out how to handle . . .

Chapter 42

Critical Point #2

UNFORTUNATELY, EVEN THE MOST POWERFUL RECOMMENDATION can run into difficulties. After we have verified the information and made a proposal to work with the prospect, we may still face a challenge.

Perhaps we'll say, "Mr. Prospect, here's our proposal, and based on what you told me last time, I think it really makes sense to work together. What do you think?" At that point the other person may well say, "Hold it. I really don't think this makes sense, and I'll tell you why." And then we may feel as though the person is throwing another head-high fastball our way.

We're not back at the opening of the call, though. If we've gathered information, verified it, and made a proposal and we then run into something that doesn't make sense to the other person, we're looking at something quite different than the instinctive negative response we heard at the beginning of the relationship. We're dealing with an issue–what most salespeople call an "objection." Actually, though, this is simply Critical Point #2 in the telephone sales process.

Issues are something that we as salespeople don't usually like to deal with, but the truth is that they are usually good signs. Issues tell us that the prospect is really listening to us, really paying attention to what we have to say about our products and services.

The main challenge for telesales professionals is not to respond too quickly or too instinctively to an issue. Often, people hear something negative and assume that there's a problem when there really isn't. Take pricing concerns, for instance. Sometimes, we're not sure exactly how to respond when the prospect says, "You're too expensive," or "I can get a better rate from ABC Company." Believe it or not, such pricing "objections" often aren't all that serious. They're closer to questions than deal-breakers.

Have you ever walked into a store to buy something like an appliance with a predetermined spending limit in mind? Have you ever exceeded that spending limit when you saw something that allowed you to do a little more than you'd initially thought you could do? I know I've done my fair share of rationalizing on this score. "Well, I'd only wanted to spend $200, but this VCR has much better recording quality than the one that's on sale for $199. It's much easier to program, too. How much more does the better model cost? $49.00? What the heck. It's worth it."

Overcome the impulse to (a) cut prices or (b) defend yourself when pricing issues arise. When a prospect or customer says, "This seems high to me," consider asking a question that will help you identify the nature of the issue. You might ask, "Well, what were you expecting?" After all, it's possible that your prospect hasn't given the question of price much thought yet and simply wants to hear more about exactly what he or she is getting for the money.

Like the initial responses of Critical Point #1, the issues we hear at Critical Point #2 can sound very imposing. The important thing is not to react emotionally or thoughtlessly, but to follow a clear process for handling the issue. First, we have to identify just what kind of issue we're dealing with. Then we have to validate that issue, typically by sharing a story or anecdote that shows how someone else we worked with overcame a similar problem. And finally, we have to solve the issue if we possibly can.

It is not always possible to solve an issue, and it's better to follow up later on a promising call than it is to promise something right now that you cannot deliver. If the prospect demands blue widgets and you only have red ones, tell the truth. Find out what you're really looking at. Acknowledge the issue in the most positive light. Then try to move on in an ethical and professional fashion. If you win a customer, that's great. If you lose a potential customer, well, that's better than losing sleep at night because you made a commitment your organization couldn't keep.

There are many different kinds of issues at Critical Point #2. Here are some of the most common:

- Product or service issues. Some of these are tougher than others. The solution to an easy problem like "We want to see a revised quote," is to respond directly to the issue the prospect has raised and avoid reselling. For a hard problem like "We want you to cancel a disputed invoice from last year," you will have to obtain help from an outside authority who can address the issue. Turn the problem over to senior management *immediately*.
- Hidden issues. This is what happens when (for instance) a prospect seems ready to buy, then suddenly stops returning your calls. Your goal is to find out what the real issue is. The best way to do this is to take personal

responsibility. In a telephone sales environment, that probably means leaving a message on the person's voice-mail system that says, essentially, "Mr. Smith, I feel I must have done something wrong. Could you please give me a call back so I can find out what it was?" You'll be amazed at how often such a person will return your call, assure you that you didn't do anything wrong, and explain what the true issue is.

- The stall. In this situation, the prospect can't move out of the "Let me run this by my people one more time" mode. Establish a timetable that works backward from the prospect's ideal date of implementation, and then articulate what has to happen in the interim. This will help you determine the appropriate decision date.
- Reassurance issues. Basically, this prospect tells you, "We've got an unusual situation, and I'm not really sure you can deliver everything you've promised." Reassurance can be a tough issue. The solution is to find out how the prospect resolved similar doubts in the past when selecting other vendors and then to supply the same kind of proof. References and testimonials can be extremely valuable in resolving reassurance issues.
- Fear, uncertainty, and doubt issues. "How many people actually use this? Will it work at all?" These kinds of issues relate to the prospect's discomfort with change. Focus on helping the person through the transition; talk about how you or someone in your organization can help get him or her started. If you can, talk about resources that can help guide the person through the initial stages (such as a portion of the company web site designed especially for initial users).

Always remember that the most common reason people don't buy is that they *do not yet want to change.* If you truly understand what the person is now doing, you will be in a good position to serve as an agent of positive change.

Action Item

Write down the most common issues you hear at Critical Point #2 of the sale. Then use the ideas in this chapter to strategize ways to *identify, validate,* and *solve* those issues.

In the next chapter, you'll learn about a secret to telephone sales success that most people ignore. Keep reading to find out . . .

Chapter 43

When to Stop Calling

A WHILE BACK, I WAS CALLED ON to help a *Fortune* 500 company improve the efficiency of its telesales force. The managers at this firm felt that their salespeople were not performing up to capacity. It was easy for me to see why the managers felt this way—group totals were down and people were missing their quotas.

After a bit of analysis, I was able to determine some fascinating things about this group's selling patterns. For one thing, the typical sale took roughly four calls to complete. After the fourth call, the odds of closing with any prospect tended to plummet. Yet these salespeople were calling their leads over and over and over again. Some people were calling individual leads ten or twenty times and counting each call as a separate dial! That's a great way to distort your calling numbers and sabotage your performance.

I told management that two things had to happen before the group could improve its numbers. First, people had to abandon the idea that calling one person twenty times counted as twenty contacts. The reps were to monitor their numbers more accurately and were to avoid calling any lead more than once a week unless that lead returned a call. And second, the team members were to *stop calling the lead if nothing had happened by the fourth call.*

Do you see why it was so important for these people to make only four calls to any given prospect? Their sales cycle demanded it! Again: When I analyzed the numbers, I found that *virtually no sales were closing on the fifth or subsequent call!* By skipping that fifth call and by avoiding the trap of calling the same leads repeatedly day after day, these salespeople would spend much more of their time connecting with new people.

The managers promised to implement my plan. When I went back to visit the company a month later, sales had jumped by 28 percent! The moral: When faced with the choice of talking to someone brand new and someone who is familiar but does not meet your criteria as a prospect, *choose to talk to someone new.*

Action Item

Reacquaint yourself with the average time cycle of your sale.

Review the material in your workbook and review Chapter 12, "The Definition of a Prospect." *Don't* call any lead more than once a week unless the lead has called you back. *Don't* call people who have failed to take action within the limits of your average selling cycle.

You're ready to tackle the final chapter of the book. It's called . . .

Chapter 44

Ten Traits of World-Class Salespeople

OVER THE YEARS, I'VE IDENTIFIED TEN TRAITS that I believe are common to the most effective salespeople—those who, by instinct, intense practice, or a combination of the two, manage to pull ahead of the pack year after year. These salespeople are the ones who tend to receive the most impressive career rewards both financially and psychologically. Here's what they have in common:

1. **They are obsessed about getting to the Next Step.** These reps know that interest is measured by commitment. That means that a prospect who agrees to meet with you again at a specific date and time is more interested in working with you than someone who says, "Let's try to talk about this sometime next quarter."

2. **They understand the importance of developing new relationships every day.** They reach out to new people every single

day—no matter what. World-class salespeople know that no one ever gets too successful to prospect. Quite the opposite: Daily commitment to an effective prospecting routine is what *makes* long-term success possible.

3. **They are focused on finding out what other people do.** Superior salespeople don't get sidetracked by what they imagine the other person "needs." Instead, they focus on learning everything they can about what other people *do* . . . and then they try to find ways to help people do what they do better.

4. **They anticipate responses.** Superior sales performers are not taken by surprise. They know how to handle the obstacles that come their way, and they prepare effective turnarounds that they deliver quickly and confidently.

5. **They understand the need to make new Initial Contacts.** Superstar salespeople realize that initial exchanges with new contacts are what turn into prospects . . . and prospects are what turn into sales. Without a stream of new face-to-face contacts with new people, every income stream eventually dries up.

6. **They count the "no" answers, not the "yes" answers.** Truly world-class salespeople realize that a certain number of "no" answers are what make any "yes" answer possible. That means each "no" answer is worth money! Superstars identify their own personal ratios—and start counting "no" answers as they collect them.

7. **They understand the necessity of verifying information.** Top salespeople understand that the quality of the information they receive gets better as their relationship with any given contact gets older. They understand the necessity of verifying everything they've learned from a contact . . . *before* making a formal presentation.

8. **They use managers and others within the organization effectively.** Superior salespeople realize that "bringing the manager into the call" or "connecting with the technical people" is an excellent way to continue a relationship with a prospect. As a

result, they're not afraid to ask others within their organization to attend second or subsequent meetings.

9. **They take the time to learn.** World-class salespeople are always on the lookout for new ways to improve themselves. Their attitude is simple: If they get just one idea they can implement profitably from a book, tape, or training program, they come out ahead of the game.

10. **They believe that they are the best.** Superstars begin with the simple, unshakable assumption that they know what they're doing and they're in a better position to help their customers than anyone else.

If you build all ten of these traits into your selling, I have no doubt that you will succeed in telesales—or in any capacity—as a salesperson.

Good luck!

Visit D.E.I. Management Group at www.dei-sales.com.

Appendix

On the following pages you will find model call sheets, sales lead tracking sheets, and daily call report sheets. Use them!

RATIOS (Outbound Calls)

Date	Dials	Completed Calls	Presentations/ Recommendations	Closed Sales

RATIOS (Outbound Calls)

Date	Dials	Completed Calls	Presentations/ Recommendations	Closed Sales

RATIOS (Outbound Calls)

Date	Dials	Completed Calls	Presentations/ Recommendations	Closed Sales

RATIOS (Outbound Calls)

Date	Dials	Completed Calls	Presentations/ Recommendations	Closed Sales

RATIOS (Inbound Calls)

Date	Calls	Issues You Can Service	Presentations/ Recommendations	Closed Sales

RATIOS (Inbound Calls)

Date	Calls	Issues You Can Service	Presentations/ Recommendations	Closed Sales

RATIOS (Inbound Calls)

Date	Calls	Issues You Can Service	Presentations/ Recommendations	Closed Sales

SALES LEAD TRACKING SHEET

Name:

Telephone:

Address:

City: State: Zip:

Contact Person:

Date	Content of call	Follow-up	Remarks

SALES LEAD TRACKING SHEET

Name:

Telephone:

Address:

City: State: Zip:

Contact Person:

Date	Content of call	Follow-up	Remarks

SALES LEAD TRACKING SHEET

Name:

Telephone:

Address:

City: State: Zip:

Contact Person:

Date	Content of call	Follow-up	Remarks

SALES LEAD TRACKING SHEET

Name:

Telephone:

Address:

City: State: Zip:

Contact Person:

Date	Content of call	Follow-up	Remarks

SALES LEAD TRACKING SHEET

Name:

Telephone:

Address:

City: State: Zip:

Contact Person:

Date	Content of call	Follow-up	Remarks

SALES LEAD TRACKING SHEET

Name:

Telephone:

Address:

City: State: Zip:

Contact Person:

Date	Content of call	Follow-up	Remarks

SALES LEAD TRACKING SHEET

Name:

Telephone:

Address:

City: State: Zip:

Contact Person:

Date	Content of call	Follow-up	Remarks

SALES LEAD TRACKING SHEET

Name:

Telephone:

Address:

City: State: Zip:

Contact Person:

Date	Content of call	Follow-up	Remarks

SALES LEAD TRACKING SHEET

Name:

Telephone:

Address:

City: State: Zip:

Contact Person:

Date	Content of call	Follow-up	Remarks

SALES LEAD TRACKING SHEET

Name:

Telephone:

Address:

City: State: Zip:

Contact Person:

Date	Content of call	Follow-up	Remarks

SALES LEAD TRACKING SHEET

Name:

Telephone:

Address:

City: State: Zip:

Contact Person:

Date	Content of call	Follow-up	Remarks

SALES LEAD TRACKING SHEET

Name:

Telephone:

Address:

City: State: Zip:

Contact Person:

Date	Content of call	Follow-up	Remarks

SALES LEAD TRACKING SHEET

Name:

Telephone:

Address:

City: State: Zip:

Contact Person:

Date	Content of call	Follow-up	Remarks

SALES LEAD TRACKING SHEET

Name:

Telephone:

Address:

City: State: Zip:

Contact Person:

Date	Content of call	Follow-up	Remarks

DAILY CALL REPORT

Date: / /

Page of

Firm name/ location	Contact name/title Telephone number	Result	Follow-up?	Prospect category

DAILY CALL REPORT

Date: / /

Page of

Firm name/ location	Contact name/title Telephone number	Result	Follow-up?	Prospect category

DAILY CALL REPORT

Date: / /

Page of

Firm name/ location	Contact name/title Telephone number	Result	Follow-up?	Prospect category

DAILY CALL REPORT

Date: / /

Page of

Firm name/ location	Contact name/title Telephone number	Result	Follow-up?	Prospect category

DAILY CALL REPORT

Date: / /

Page of

Firm name/ location	Contact name/title Telephone number	Result	Follow-up?	Prospect category

DAILY CALL REPORT

Date: / /

Page of

Firm name/ location	Contact name/title Telephone number	Result	Follow-up?	Prospect category

DAILY CALL REPORT

Date: / /

Page of

Firm name/ location	Contact name/title Telephone number	Result	Follow-up?	Prospect category

TRACKING SHEET

Dials	Discussions	Presentations	Sales

TRACKING SHEET

Dials	Discussions	Presentations	Sales

TRACKING SHEET

Dials	Discussions	Presentations	Sales

TRACKING SHEET

Dials	Discussions	Presentations	Sales

TRACKING SHEET

Dials	Discussions	Presentations	Sales

TRACKING SHEET

Dials	Discussions	Presentations	Sales

Index

A

B

C

D

L

M

N

O

P

About the Author

STEPHAN SCHIFFMAN is a certified management consultant and the founder of D.E.I. Management Group, one of the country's fastest-growing sales training companies. Mr. Schiffman has helped over 500,000 professionals become more successful through a variety of selling and coaching seminars. He has been named by *Selling Power* magazine the country's pre-eminent expert on sales prospecting. Mr. Schiffman is the author of *Cold Calling Techniques (That Really Work!)* and many other popular business books; he is a frequent guest on national radio and television programs. To learn more about Stephan Schiffman or D.E.I. Management Group, call 1-800-224-2140 or visit *www.dei-sales.com.*

Also by Stephan Schiffman

Power Sales Presentations

A step-by-step guide to preparing and delivering powerful sales presentations. Includes examples of real-life dialogues that show you what *not* to say, and how to respond to a prospect's questions or comments. *Power Sales Presentations* provides an overview of the entire in-person selling process for sales professionals in all industries. It is the perfect companion to the author's more specialized books on cold calling and telemarketing.

ISBN: 1-55850-252-1
Trade paperback
$7.95, 208 pages

Closing Techniques (That Really Work!), 2nd Edition

"Closing the sale" is the part of the job nearly every salesperson dreads, yet it can actually be the easiest part of the sales cycle. Sales trainer Stephan Schiffman shows how to integrate the closing process into a productive, professional sales cycle—and turn prospects into allies, not adversaries. He focuses on helping, not pressuring, the customer. His innovative system makes manipulative tricks and high-pressure techniques obsolete.

ISBN: 1-58062-172-4
Trade paperback
$8.95, 160 pages

The Consultant's Handbook, 2nd Edition

The definitive resource for those who want to enter one of today's most exciting, challenging, and potentially lucrative career fields—consulting. *The Consultant's Handbook* provides an authoritative, balanced appraisal of the benefits as well as the pitfalls you can expect to encounter in this dynamic field.

ISBN: 1-58062-441-3
Trade paperback
$12.95, 192 pages

Also by Stephan Schiffman

Cold Calling Techniques (That Really Work!), 4th Edition

Cold Calling Techniques is the ultimate guide to creating new sales—one of the most critical skills salespeople need. This new edition features the same basic message—if you want to increase your sales, you must get good at cold calling to get the face-to-face appointments you need. Stephan Schiffman also teaches the latest innovations in sales training and explains new technologies.

ISBN: 1-58062-076-0
Trade paperback
$8.95, 160 pages

The 25 Sales Habits of Highly Successful Salespeople, 2nd Edition

Demonstrates how most successful salespeople practice powerful, effective sales techniques—and shows you how to make these techniques part of your own set of selling skills. From tips on developing selling plans to strategies for getting quality referrals, Schiffman's advice can help you sell more. Stephan Schiffman's techniques are practical, relevant, and easy to apply.

ISBN: 1-55850-391-9
Trade paperback
$6.95, 128 pages

The 25 Most Common Sales Mistakes (and How to Avoid Them), 2nd Edition

Are you losing sales you should have made? Most salespeople are! Why? They make fundamental mistakes—ranging from failing to really listen to potential clients to failing to stay in touch after a sale. Stephan Schiffman's clear, concise, easy-to-use handbook shows you how to identify and correct these costly errors.

ISBN: 1-55850-511-3
Trade paperback
$6.95, 128 pages

Also by Stephan Schiffman

25 Sales Skills They Don't Teach at Business School

In the latest book in his successful *25 Sales* series, Schiffman provides practical answers to 25 important questions facing the business professional today—questions ranging from simple office etiquette to learning how to recognize and handle a negotiation dead end. He addresses how to get prospects to open up, the 10 most common sales mistakes and how to avoid them, what to do when you are shot down in a sales meeting, and more!

ISBN: 1-58062-614-9
Trade paperback
$6.95, 128 pages

The 25 Sales Strategies That Will Boost Your Sales Today!

More great advice from Stephan Schiffman! He reveals 25 sales-building strategies that he's developed and tested during his years of training top-notch salespeople. And he provides clear explanations of proven, practical strategies, such as: learning how to build interdependent relationships with your customers; listening to your prospects for clues on how to move the sales process forward; and working with your customers to find new uses for your product or service.

ISBN: 1-58062-116-3
Trade paperback
$6.95, 128 pages

Available Wherever Books Are Sold

If you cannot find these titles at your favorite retail outlet, you may order them directly from the publisher. BY PHONE: Call 1-800-872-5627. We accept Visa, MasterCard, American Express, and Discover. $4.95 will be added to your total order for shipping and handling. BY MAIL: Write out the full titles of the books you'd like to order and send payment, including $4.95 for shipping and handling, to: Adams Media Corporation, 57 Littlefield Street, Avon, MA 02322. 30-day money-back guarantee.